Tales from the
Council Chamber

by
Olive Brown
and
Chris Foote Wood

NORTHERN WRITERS

First published in 2009 by Northern Writers "Wor Hoos" 28 Cockton Hill Road Bishop Auckland County Durham DL14 6AH www.writersinc.biz

British Library Cataloguing in Publication Data
A catalogue for this book is available from the British Library.

ISBN 978-0-9553869-6-1

Produced & Edited by Chris Foote Wood at footewood@btconnect.com
Cartoons by ROG - Roger Bowles at rogcartoons@madasafish.com

Typeset in 10/12pt Times
Typesetting and origination, printed and bound by Lintons Printers Ltd, Beechburn, Crook, Co Durham DL15 8RA
www.lintons-printers.co.uk

To the People of Wear Valley

Contents

FOREWORD

The two of us have been political opponents for many years, but we have readily and happily combined to write this book. The reason is simple: for all our political differences, we both have a lifetime motivation to represent and serve the people of Wear Valley. Apart from belonging to two different political parties, we have much in common: we have both been long-serving District Councillors, both are now Honorary Aldermen, both of us have been Chairman and Leader of the Council and Leader of our respective Council Groups, both of us have been members of the North East Assembly and the EU Committee of the Regions, and both of us have been active in the Town Twinning movement. In more general terms, we both have an international outlook, we both love travel and books. And we have both been betrayed by members of our own parties, each of us being removed from office by the secret machinations of others in our Party.

This book is in no way intended to be a complete history of our time in local government. Many significant individuals and important events are not recorded here. A full account of our combined 77 years on Wear Valley District Council would require a massive tome, it would be far too expensive to produce and would not be an entertaining read – which we hope you will find within these pages. We do record some serious matters in this book, but for the most part we have brought you an amusing and we hope interesting series of anecdotes and stories that have enriched our lives, and which we now pass on to you.

Olive Brown and Chris Foote Wood
of Crook and Bishop Auckland, respectively, in the District of Wear Valley in the County of Durham, North East England.

March 2009

HONOURS BOARD

Wear Valley District Council 1973-2009

Olive Brown MBE

Crook & Willington UD Councillor 1970-74

Wear Valley DC Councillor 1973-2007

Chairman of the Council 1981-82

Leader of the Council 1995-2005

Labour Group Leader 1995-2005

Appointed Hon. Alderman 2007

Chris Foote Wood

Bishop Auckland UD Councillor 1967-74

Wear Valley DC Councillor 1973-2007

Chairman of the Council 1976-77

Leader of the Council 1976-79, 1991-94

Liberal/LibDem Group Leader 1972-1994, 1995-2006

Appointed Hon. Alderman 2007

"Have you got a family?"

Chapter One

Chris: How I came to Bishop

"Have you got a family?"; "What position do you play?"; A pound short;
A diplomatic incident; "Help yersel' hinney"; The Demon Drink;
Down South; "Sheer Cheek"

"Have you got a family?"
I strode into the Council Chamber with all the confidence of youth. This was
Ashington Town Hall, home of the local urban district council. I was looking for
a job, my first job, any job. The fact was that I was unemployed, I was married
with a child on the way and my wife, still a student, was on her last year at
King's College, Newcastle. I had left there a few weeks earlier, having
completed a four-year honours degree course in civil engineering but without a
degree. So I needed a job, and I needed it badly. I had done my homework, but
on entering the traditional Council Chamber with its circular rows of seats like
some miniature Roman amphitheatre, my heart sank. Ranged against me was
Ashington Council. Not just some of the Council, but all of them, the whole lot.
Yes, in those days the full Council, every Member, sat in on the appointment of
even the most humblest of council staff. And I was hopefully about to become
the humblest of their staff, namely a junior assistant engineer. After all, I didn't
have a degree, so what else could I expect?

It seemed to me that every one of these Councillors was an old man. Possibly
some of them were middle-aged. They were all either miners or ex-miners. 95%
of local men either worked or had worked at the Ashington-Woodhorn complex,
then the largest deep coal-mine in Europe. I don't recall any women Councillors,
although there may have been one or two. So all my earlier plans about showing
how clever I was went out of the window. In the event, the venerable and
distinguished (so it seemed to me) Councillors asked me only two questions -
two questions which I found all too easy to answer. The first question was:
'Have you got a family?' I answered in the affirmative. 'Yes, we got married last
year and there's a baby on the way'. The venerable and distinguished
Councillors, family men to a man, smiled and nodded. They had all been
through it, raised a family, and no doubt had had hard times too. They
appreciated that a young chap like me, with a wife and a baby on the way,
needed a job – badly.

"What position do you play?"

The second question was more tricky, but I was prepared. Even so, it came as a surprise. 'What position do you play?' was the question. What they meant was, what position did I play in a football team, because here in Ashington, the home of the Milburns and the Charltons, there was only one sport that really mattered, and that was football. But I had done my homework. I'd been at the Council offices during the day, and had made searching enquiries as to what the Councillors would be looking for. The answer surprised me – they were looking for a left-winger. Now I know I'm radical in my views, but I'm no Communist and never have been. And Labour councillors in the North East were notorious for their right-wing views. But I was soon put right. 'They're looking for a left-winger for the Council soccer team,' I was told – equally surprising, but true. The Councillors were inordinately proud of the Ashington Council football team, and they would enquire closely as to its progress. When told the side was short of a left-winger, then the next staff appointment, a left-winger – in the football sense – had to be found.

As it happens, I did play football – not very cleverly, mind – and, being left-footed, I genuinely did play left-wing. Or, as the saying is: 'first I was left-wing, then left-half, then left-back, then left-out'. I was not a clever football player, having very few skills in that department. But I was keen, I would run all day and do my best. So I simply answered 'yes, I play left-wing'. I did not claim to be much of a player, so I didn't tell any lies. And that was it. No more questions – just the two, which I had answered satisfactorily. Outside, I couldn't imagine what the result would be, but soon enough I was called back in. The job was mine! Apparently, my main rival was single. He didn't have a family. As to his football prowess, I never inquired. And that was the start of my relatively short career as a Local Government Officer, which I gave up to become a Councillor. Oh yes, I did play for the Ashington Council soccer team, at left-wing. And we did get to the semi-finals of the NALGO County Cup, so honour was satisfied.

A pound short

I enjoyed my time working for Ashington UDC. In those days – this was 1962 – these little local councils 'did everything'. A small urban council was an efficient working unit, small-scale and local. But I wasn't concerned about that - I was desperate for my first pay. My wife was still a university student, I'd been out of work since leaving college and we were really stretched. Ashington UDC employees were paid every Thursday fortnight, cash from the Co-op Bank, a week in arrears. That was the rule. So it was three weeks all but a day when I climbed the stairs to the Treasurer's office, eager to get my hands on my first pay packet. On the first floor landing there was a tiny reception area, devoid of furniture. Facing you was a small window with a grill such as you used to find in cinemas or fairgrounds. Above was a notice. In stern tones it said: *'Check your wages before leaving, as mistakes cannot be rectified'*. I approached the tiny window with some trepidation. It was the Council Treasurer himself who sat behind the grill and doled out the money as if every penny was his own. Behind the Treasurer you could see a couple of clerks – both men - sitting at high desks, Bob Cratchit style, with their dippy-in pens writing up these huge ledgers. It was like a scene from Charles Dickens' Christmas Carol. I gave my name, drew my pay packet and checked its contents carefully. I was a pound short!

"A pound short"

Now my pay in those days was six pounds 12 shillings and 8 pence a week. But I definitely seemed to be one pound short. No matter which way I looked at it, on the top line, instead of saying thirteen pound odd for two week's salary, it said 12 pound odd - definitely a pound short. So I went back to the little opening with even greater trepidation than before. 'What do you want?' demanded the Treasurer. I felt like Oliver Twist, asking for more. Well, I was asking for more, but only what was due to me. 'Please sir, I seem to be a pound short'. For once in my life, my voice trembled. 'Give it here,' demanded the Treasurer, snatching my pay packet from me. He examined it closely for a few seconds before tossing it back down on the counter in front of me. 'There's nothing wrong with that,' he said. I said no, but the more I protested, the more he was adamant. But I just would not give in. I wanted that pound! I needed that pound – badly! The Treasurer sighed before giving me the coup-de-grace with a deadly thrust. 'Tell me, young man, when did you start your employment with this Authority?' I replied it was on Monday the such-and-such date. The Treasurer smiled a smile of deadly satisfaction. 'Exactly. You started on a Monday. We start our week on a Sunday, and you weren't here on the Sunday'. With that, he threw my pay packet down again and closed the hatch. I was beat - and a pound short.

In the interim I had got to know my workmates, and a very fine bunch of lads they were too. But my boss, the Council Engineer and Surveyor, was to me a distant figure of authority. As far as I can recall, he never ever came into the drawing office. When he wanted someone to attend him in his office, he would ring the bell. One ring for the deputy, two for the chief assistant, three for the senior assistant and so forth. As the lowliest person there, it was seven rings for me. I think there was only one occasion when the bell rang seven times. I hurried round to the great man's door, knocked and went in on his command. 'Who are you?" he demanded. I told him. He snorted: 'I didn't ring for you, I rang for Craggs. Send him in'. What had happened was, the boss had forgotten how many times he had rung the bell, so he rang it a couple of times more, just to be sure.

A diplomatic incident

There was another occasion on which the boss's bell sounded drama. It was after lunch. Now the boss did like a drink at lunch time, not to excess, you understand, but he certainly enjoyed his social life. On this occasion we were all hard at it after our dinners when the bell rang - one, long, continuous ring. It was for the deputy, and it was clearly urgent. Voices were raised, doors opened and closed, telephones rang, people ran hither and thither. Later, the deputy came into the drawing office to explain what had happened. 'The boss has just sacked half a dozen Electric men,' he said. Apparently our boss was returning from his lunch, when he spotted some workmen standing idly by a hole in the road, leaning on their shovels. He leapt out of his car and stormed over. 'You men, you are all sacked!' he trumpeted, and with that, he jumped back into his car and drove off. These men were working for the Electricity Board (NEEB), not the Council, and it took all the diplomatic skills of our deputy to sort it out without too many repercussions. This reminds me of a tale told during WW2. A senior civil servant went in to see the Minister of Supply. 'There's a great shortage of shovels for the men working on the roads, Minister, what's to be done?' The Minister thought for a moment. 'There's only one thing for it,' he said, 'if they can't lean on their shovels, they'll just have to lean on each other'

"You're all sacked!"

"Help yersel' hinney"

After the birth of our first child – my son Nicolas - Ashington Council gave us the tenancy of a little flat, and the three of us moved in. Ashington people are very kind and very welcoming, but they do want to know all your business – and I mean all. The elderly couple in the bungalow on one side of us were aghast when they found out that we didn't get any free coal. As a matter of fact we did get some, as my father-in-law was a miner and he gave us some of his allocation, but it wasn't a lot. The old couple took me to one side. 'Listen, son, we've got mair coal than we ivvor need. It's aal free. So divvent even ask, help yersel' to

9

"A pail o'coals"

a pail o' coals, hinney, onnytime you like'. Although their coal was indeed free, and they did have more than they needed, this was a generous gesture. Our other neighbour in the next door flat also wanted to be hospitable, but his idea of hospitality was to take me down to his local club and get me drunk.

The Demon Drink
You must understand in Ashington in those days, there were three pubs and twenty-seven clubs. The reason for that is that the town had originally been "dry" – it was built on Church land - and the only way the miners could get a drink would be at the club or go to one of the pubs on the edge of town. My neighbour belonged to the Buffs Club. 'You should come down some night,' he said, 'You should be a member'. Now at that time I was completely teetotal. Like my dear Mother, in her youth an active member of the Rechabites, not a

drop of alcohol had ever passed my lips, not even at Christmas. It does now, mind, and I strongly deny that I'm trying to make up for lost time. But at that time I was strictly a non-drinker as far as the booze was concerned, so I didn't fancy going down to the Buffs Club, or any other club for that matter and stand among a bunch of miners to ask for a lime and lemon. So I made every excuse not to go. Eventually my neighbour pressed me hard as to why I wouldn't come, so I decided to tell him why. 'I'm teetotal, absolutely teetotal,' I said, 'I don't drink. Atall'. This didn't put him off in the slightest. He couldn't see any reason why I should not accompany him to the club. 'We have a lad down the club,' he replied, 'he's teetotal. In fact, if he drinks four pints a night, it's a lot'. There's no answer to that!

Down South

But my time in Ashington was limited. I was ambitious to do my best for my family, and like so many North-Easterners before me, I thought I would try my luck Down South. So I got a job with Guildford Borough Council at twice the wage I was earning at Ashington. But that too was a mistake. I had jumped out of the frying-pan into the fire. Although my wages had doubled, the cost of living in the South even then was much greater than in the North. We were ambitious to buy our own home, and the price of houses in posh and well-heeled Guildford put one well beyond our reach. A work colleague suggested I follow his example and build my own house, and he took me along to show me the site where he was building his new home. I was very impressed. 'How much is this costing you?' I asked. He replied it was ten thousand pounds. 'That's a lot,' I said, 'to pay for a house' [this was 1964]. 'That's not for the house,' he said, 'that's just for the plot'. So the first chance I got, I came back to the North East. And that's how we landed in Bishop Auckland, where a perfectly good house could be obtained for around a thousand pounds. I have three sisters and three children. All six also tried their luck down South. Three stayed, and three came back North. And my dear wife Frances is from London – but that's another story.

"Sheer Cheek"

My interview in Bishop Auckland Town Hall was a complete contrast to the one I had had at Ashington. Instead of the full Council, there were only three men there, and only one was a Councillor. It was my sheer good luck that that one man was Cllr Harold Stephenson, a leading member of the Civic Group on the Council. Instead of the Labour Party, the Civics – a collection of non-Labour councillors - were in control. Harold's two companions were Fred Mole, the Engineer & Surveyor, and his deputy Derrick Graham. Fred was a gentleman, quietly spoken. Derrick was just as much a gentleman, but even more quietly spoken. So you can take it that Harold, who had built up his own massive construction firm from small beginnings, did most of the talking. This time the interview was more technical, but only as far as Fred was concerned, and then with only one such question. 'How many yards to the gulley?' Fred asked. He meant how many square yards of roadway to one gulley. I knew the correct answer and gave it confidently. Fred was satisfied.

"Sheer cheek"

But that was not the end of it. There were seven of us candidates for interview. Although I was first to be asked back into the interview room and was indeed offered the job, it was at the bottom of the scale – little more than I'd been earning at Ashington. So, with six other people waiting outside – there was much unemployment at the time - I said I would not accept the job unless it was at the top of the scale. Out I went once more to await my fate. To my surprise, I was asked in again. 'We'll give you the job, but next to the top of the scale, which you'll reach next year anyway,' said Harold. I accepted. Any other outcome would have seen me settle somewhere else in the North East, and my 40 years as a Bishop Auckland councillor would never have happened. Years later, I asked Harold why he gave me the job. 'Sheer cheek,' he said.

Chapter Two

Olive: Starting Out

*Early life; My friend from Belgium; Topping the Poll;
"A nice little girl!"; Barbara Wilkinson*

Early life

Olive: I was born in Crook where I still live. My family was very well known in the town. I went to Crook Infants school and passed the eleven-plus to go to Wolsingham Grammar School where I stayed for six years. There I won prizes for history and chemistry. I could have gone on to higher education, but I decided I didn't want to go to college and instead I looked for a job. Because of my love of books, I went into the library service where I made many friends. I worked in Crook library, but also went to the libraries at Stanhope, Wolsingham and Tow Law, as well as going out with the Durham County Council travelling library. Little did I know that all these areas were going to be a part of Wear Valley District Council!

In 1961 I met my husband Ken at a dance in Darlington. We married the following year. Ken is the "strong silent type" - a perfect foil for me. He stands for no nonsense and we've had a very happy marriage. A serious operation meant I couldn't have any children. Naturally this upset me very much, but having no children was perhaps another reason for becoming involved in politics. The Labour Party meetings at Crook were held in the old library in the Mechanics Institute where I used to work, but is now demolished. I decided to go to one of the meetings and joined the Party.

My friend from Belgium

This is how I met my life-long friend Diane De Maeyer. Ken and I had been married only a year or so when we took a coach trip to Ostend in Belgium, booked through a local travel agent. We were met at the hotel in Ostend by this young Belgian woman who was to be our tour guide. She and I hit it off straight away, and we have been close friends ever since, visiting one another regularly. Like me, Diane has an international outlook. Her mother was half Italian, and Diane made her career in the travel business, first as a courier and then with her own travel bureau, organising school trips. She was a member of the Belgian Labour Party, and it was in fact Diane who encouraged me to join the Labour Party and become active in politics, so she has a lot to answer for! Ken and I have walked in many May Day parades in Belgium.

I learned to speak French at Wolsingham Grammar School and passed my GCE 'O' level in French with flying colours. I also learned to speak German, but not at school. I went to night classes in Crook. This proved very useful on my first trip to our twin town of Bad Oeynhausen in Germany. The family we stayed with did not speak a word of English, so it was German or nothing. Fortunately my German quickly came back to me and soon I was not only conversing fluently, but also translating on many formal and informal occasions. I helped set up the voluntary-run Wear Valley Twinning Association with Bad Oeynhausen. The Council called a public meeting to set up the Association. Charles Marshall was elected chairman with me as deputy chairman. Jean Cowing was secretary and Cllr Tommy Hall was on the committee. My love of languages also stood me in good stead when I became a member of the EU Committee of the Regions.

Topping the Poll
The elections for Crook & Willington district council were due in 1970 and I thought I might as well put my name forward. There was talk that the government was going to reorganise local councils and make them bigger, but we didn't know that this was going to be the last election for the Crook & Willington council. I was selected to represent Crook East ward for the Labour Party. In those days Crook East was a three-seat ward with three councillors. The election count was most exciting, not least because I topped the poll. Second place went to Tom Lauder who was an Independent candidate, so he was also declared elected, but it was very close for the third position between the other two Labour candidates, Violet Crooks and Hetty Johnson. After several recounts the result was a tie. It was decided that they could either draw straws or toss a coin. Both agreed to toss a coin, Violet Crooks called correctly and was duly elected. I had never been involved in anything like that before, and to have that experience in my first election was rather unique. We've had many election recounts since then, but nothing like that when it was a tie after numerous recounts. I was one of the youngest Councillors to be elected to the Council. There were two men who were also quite young, so we were making inroads.

"A nice little girl!"
My first council meeting is something I will never forget. As a newly-elected, young woman councillor, I thought I was "the bees knees". Going to the meeting, I wore a Russian-type coat with fur around the bottom. It was an evening meeting, and quite cold, but I wanted to look smart. As I walked into the Council Chamber, a man's voice said: 'By, you're a nice little girl, we didn't expect a nice little girl like you to be elected to the Council'. I thought: 'Oh dear, I don't know what to make of this,' but that remark struck a chord with me and

I've never forgotten it. In fact, I think it made me more determined than ever that I had to succeed on my own merits, and not because I was "a nice little girl" or a woman for that matter. That one careless remark really shaped my thoughts about women being involved in politics. I thought: 'ok, I might be a nice little girl, but this nice little girl can also be a little toughie'.

A nice little girl!

I enjoyed my four years on Crook & Willington council. I was on several committees, and after a while I became Chairman of the Estates, Properties & Public Lighting Committee [Chris: I held a similar position on Bishop Auckland Council at the same time]. This committee dealt with all the land and facilities that the Council owned, parks, recreation grounds, cemeteries etc, so I was right at the centre of things. I quite enjoyed it, becoming a chairman was different and great experience. I learned the foundations of how to chair meetings, and I saw how councils are run, or not run, as the case may be.

Barbara Wilkinson
Before I got onto Crook & Willington Council, there was a furore over Independent Councillor Barbara Wilkinson from Willington. At the time,

Barbara was the only opposition member of the Council, but she was a tough character and not easily overawed. She is in fact the only person ever to beat JR (John Richardson) in a local election when she defeated him for a seat on Durham County Council. It was a fact in those days that many of the Labour Councillors had relatives working for the Council, but they always declared an interest when the appointments were made. Edie Wragg had two sons and several nieces and nephews on the Council staff, and she was always having to declare an interest when jobs or promotions came up.

This happened quite often, and Barbara Wilkinson didn't like it. She got so annoyed at one meeting when Mrs Wragg again "declared an interest" for the umpteenth time, that she jumped up and said: 'instead of Cllr Mrs Wragg continually declaring an interest, wouldn't it be quicker if she told us which of her relatives is NOT working for the Council?' There was hell on, Barbara Wilkinson was thrown out of the meeting and later made to apologise, but no other action was taken against her. It might have been a touch embarrassing.

Chapter Three

Chris: Working for the Council

First Class Boss; Breach of Protocol; I become Fred's boss; Category "D",
Party Leaders, Lord Shuttleworth

First Class Boss

When I did eventually become a Councillor on that same Council and took over
the same position that Harold held, that is Chairman of the Works, Estates &
Property committee, it became my job to interview staff, along with Fred. I
discovered that Fred only ever did ever ask job applicants one question, and it
was always the same question: 'how many yards to the gulley?' Fred reckoned
that anybody that did know this basic fact of council engineering would fit the
job, and anybody who didn't know it would not. But don't get me wrong, Fred
Mole was a first class Engineer and Surveyor. For a start, Fred was adamant that
the old railway viaduct at Newton Cap – despite the contrary opinion by the
County Engineer - would carry a new road. Later on, Fred was totally vindicated
when the County Council engineers had to change their minds and admit that
yes, the viaduct was strong enough to carry a new road, when for years and years
they had been saying that it wasn't. So Fred was right all along, and I'm not
surprised.

Another thing about Fred was that he was determined to improve conditions
throughout the District. When I started work as his senior assistant engineer,
Fred took me into his office and into his confidence. He showed me a map of the
District. He pointed out all the things that needed doing: all the ash closets to be
done away with, the remaining back-to-back houses to be improved; water and
sewage supply to be linked up to every little hamlet – some were still isolated in
that respect - and to make up all the many unmade private streets. Under his
direction, we were to draw up plans to put all these things right – a far-sighted
and ambitious programme for a small District Council to undertake. Fred did
this from his own conviction. He knew the Council, of whatever political colour,
wanted to see the District improved, but Fred didn't wait for instructions from
the Council. He was strongly motivated himself, and he would put forward plans
for improvement of his own accord. In other words, he was pro-active, and I
loved him for it. As well as that, Fred was a wonderful boss to work for. He
never ever criticised you or raised his voice, he was always polite, and he would
ask you, request you to do a job, not tell you. And once he had given you a job
to do, he would let you get on with it, only requiring you to report back to him
at intervals. We were a small urban council which carried out the majority of

17

functions within its borders with its own small staff, in my mind, the most efficient way of providing local services, but that's just my opinion, and I suppose I am biased. But not every senior member of staff was as good to me as Fred. Being young, keen, and pro-active, I tended to stray across the boundaries of what was acceptable in local government.

Breach of Protocol

On one occasion I found that one of my plans was being held up because of a delay in the Clerk's Department. We engineers were based in The Elms, just across from the Town Hall. I walked over past the main building to Old Bank Chambers where the Clerk's department was situated. I went up to the first-floor office of the Deputy Clerk whose job it was to clear these plans. I knocked and went in. On hearing my request as to how my plan was progressing, the Deputy Clerk was utterly appalled. Jumping up, he admonished me severely. 'If you have a problem, you see your boss Mr Mole. Mr Mole then talks to my boss, Mr Passey, and then Mr Passey talks to me. That's the way to do it. And don't ever, ever come into this department again with a request like this. Go through the proper channels'. With that I returned to The Elms with my tail between my legs.

"Ordered out"

I become Fred's boss

There were scores of unmade streets throughout the District (and still are) and these "Private Street Works" schemes to upgrade them proved a turning point for me. Under Fred Mole's instructions I prepared plans to do up eight or ten streets at a time. But of course, there is always red tape. These plans had to be approved by the County Court. It only needed one resident to object, and if so there was a problem, a delay at least. And so it proved. The very first private street scheme we took to the court was thrown out because of a single objection. That was enough for Fred. I was told to pack up those plans and get on with something else. I believe some of those plans are still sitting on the shelves to this very day. It was frustrating for me to work on a scheme and then to find out it wasn't going to be carried out. It wasn't Fred's fault, not at all, but that was why I started to feel that I could get more done if I actually became a Councillor. And when I did, and became Chairman of the Works committee, I was, at least nominally, in charge of my old boss Fred Mole. But Fred didn't mind, he treated me exactly the same as he had done when I was his senior engineer. Fred was a wonderful man, and typical of many professionals who were motivated to work in the service of the public entirely by a sense of duty.

Category "D"

One of the jobs I did for Bishop Auckland UDC was to survey the village of Witton Park prior to its complete demolition under the County Council's now infamous Category "D" policy. As I measured every street, every house, every outhouse and every ash closet, I began to wonder why on earth anyone would want to destroy a complete village (and indeed 120 others throughout County Durham) when it was abundantly clear that this was a settled, thriving community with all facilities to hand. All that was needed was for the houses that needed improvement to be renovated and brought up to modern standards, and for the unmade streets to be made up. A few houses no doubt were "too far gone" and would have had to be demolished anyway, but the great majority were perfectly capable of improvement at a modest cost. This would have been far cheaper than total demolition and building new homes, especially as many of the new houses turned out to be of inferior quality and – what an irony – had to be demolished themselves after a few years(!)

But it was the people that had the biggest impact on me. They were open, friendly and welcoming. I could have spent all day drinking cups of tea. I decided I could not be part of what I later came to realise was a crime against humanity, the deliberate destruction of living, thriving communities by the very Councillors that the people themselves had elected. Category "D" was being implemented by the County and District Councils. All the protests came to nothing, and so for me the only solution was to bring about a change of policy by those councils, and the only way to do that was to remove Labour from its decades-long monopoly of power. So I quit the Council and got a job as Bridge and Section Engineer on the Durham A1(M) Motorway construction.

Party Leaders

Two Liberal/LibDem Leaders have visited Category "D" villages in my area at my request. Jeremy Thorpe, an outstanding personality who was brought down by homophobia and the stupidity of his so-called friends, came to Binchester around 1973/74. He made a fantastic impact with the local people and was intrigued to find himself in Gladstone Street. In later life Thorpe, while retaining his considerable mental faculties, has suffered from a debilitating disease. Frances and I were both pleased and sad to see him at his home some while ago, together with his wife who cares for him devotedly. Paddy Ashdown had a look round the Dene Valley Villages and spent some time on the allotments near Close House, talking to the lads who keep trotting horses. Paddy was fascinated, and talked enthusiastically of "half bred" and "quarter bred" horses.

Lord Shuttleworth

The purpose of these visits was not for publicity, but to show our Party Leaders first hand just what a crime Category "D" was. I did the same with Lord Shuttleworth, and with great effect. Lord Shuttleworth – a Tory grandee who described himself as "just a sheep farmer" (he owned a large part of Cumbria) – was the Chairman of the Rural Development Commission. We had applied for large parts of the District to be given "Priority Rural Development Area" status, thus qualifying for major grant aid for these former coalfield areas. The civil servants in London were giving us a hard time, refusing even to consider the Dene Valley because the ward included the South Church Industrial Estate. The way the (highly paid) Westminster mandarins saw it, you couldn't give Rural Development Area status to an industrial estate – and you couldn't "split" a ward. This was of course complete nonsense, but it needed someone of Lord Shuttleworth's status to knock heads together.

So I said to Lord Shuttleworth: "next time you come up to Newcastle, get your car to divert through the Dene Valley. You don't even have to get out of the car – just look around you as you drive through." This he did, and lo and behold we got our special status for the Dene Valley and all the rest followed. Without this special status, there would have been no grants and no redevelopment. Later, after we had gained an initial £500,000 grant (for six villages over five years, not a lot) thanks to WVDC Council planner Bob Hope and my LibDem colleague Cllr Geoff Harrison who made the presentation, the same civil servants were refusing to hand over the cash – they called it "drawing down". I happened to meet Lord Shuttleworth in London, and told him about it. Again he knocked heads together, and we got our first instalment within days. I speak as I find, and I thought Lord Shuttleworth did a great job as Chairman of the RDA. Unlike so many of his ilk who are appointed to these high-flying positions, he genuinely understood the problems and was enthusiastic about the job and making it work. Yet in 1997 he was sacked by the incoming Labour government, a dreadful decision. The RDA was abolished and its functions split between several other bodies who in my opinion have not been half as effective as the RDA.

It's a sad fact that these battles have to be fought to get any form of progress, especially in the Category "D" villages which were denied any form of public investment for decades after initially being condemned to be bulldozed completely. But it's also very hard to explain to the local residents who see only the injustice they have suffered and vent their frustration on the very people – like me – who are only trying to help them. How you make sense of a local council election when your opponents are chanting "Get the Tories Out!" and "Vote for Tony Blair" is a mystery to me, especially when (a) this is a local election, and (b) there are no Tories standing in my ward. The day after one council election in 1995, a man in Eldon Lane shouted at me "Why isn't Tony Blair in Downing Street?" He genuinely thought he'd been voting in a General Election!

Chapter Four

Olive: Fighting for a Principle

Standing against Labour; Back in the Party; "Them Over the Water"

Standing against Labour

The much-talked about local government reorganisation came into being in 1974. Elections to these new councils were held in 1973, so we had a "shadow year" with the old Councils continuing on, before the new Wear Valley District Council took over. Wear Valley was an amalgamation of four local councils, the urban districts of Crook & Willington, Bishop Auckland and Tow Law, and Weardale rural district council. Again I thought I would throw my hat into the ring and stand for the new Wear Valley Council. However, I must have made a few enemies in the Party, although I wasn't aware of it at the time. When it came to the selection of candidates for the new Council. I lost out by one vote. It was only later that we found out that some people who voted didn't live in the ward. One chap who voted at the meeting lived at Sunnyside, three or four miles away and totally out of my ward. I only lost by one vote and I was really furious about it. A young Councillor from Hunwick, Donald White, was having similar problems to me. He lost his nomination by only one or two of votes, and he felt the same as me. We decided to appeal against the decision.

People in my ward were urging me to stand and I said there would be no point unless I got elected. They came back with things like 'we are going to see that you get in because it's totally wrong. You've done a good job and people are satisfied with you. You're young, you've lived in Crook all your life and you know what people want in the town'. And so I decided to stand as a "People's Representative" against the official Labour Party candidate. As it turned out, I was elected by a huge majority. This really pleased me. The people of Crook had turned out to support me, as they have done every since - bless them! Don White was also elected as an Independent for Hunwick, beating the official Labour candidate. It didn't matter to me that Don and I were not in a political party. I was excited about being elected and proving a point to people.

Back in the Party

Going to that first meeting of the new Wear Valley Council at Glenholme in 1973, I was apprehensive. I thought the Labour councilors were going to be really horrible to me and Don White, but fortunately they weren't. Donald and I just sat in the Council Chamber and took what we were given as regards committee places, which wasn't a lot but we accepted that. The Liberals were trying to persuade Donald and I to cross the floor, but we didn't. I wanted to prove a point that I was still with the Labour Party, although they were not with me at that time. After a few months, we got word back that because of all that had happened we had to be asked to go back into the Labour Party. That pleased me a lot. We had proved our point, and we were right because we weren't selected properly in the first place. So at the end of the day I went back into the Labour Party. I was glad because I have always enjoyed being involved with the Party.

1973 was also the year I became a magistrate. That thrilled me a lot as well. I thought it was another string to my bow, as I was very interested in the law. I really enjoyed my time on the bench at Bishop Auckland. Being a magistrate is completely different to being a Councillor. On that front, Wear Valley took a lot of "bedding in" because it consisted of four smaller councils, each one very different. Wear Valley is very diverse, large in area but small in population - we have more sheep than people - but it was an interesting set-up.

"Them Over the Water"
Fortunately for me, I knew a lot of the people from Weardale because of my work with the library service, so I knew most of the Councillors from Weardale and Tow Law. I didn't know many people from Bishop Auckland, so that was a bit of a problem. I did know Conservative councillor Margaret Hurst because she was a magistrate, and I knew Liberal councillor Chris Wood, as he was then. I quickly became familiar with the Labour members from Bishop Auckland, as we soon realised we had to work together. Although I enjoyed my first year as a Wear Valley councillor, it was very difficult because people always tended to think of their own local area rather than the District as a whole. But you have to look at the larger picture, and when I became Leader of the Council I made a vow that I was going to do away with this "them and us" situation. "Them over the water" is how some Crook & Willington councillors described the Bishop Auckland members – and vice versa.

Chapter Five

Chris: Why don't you stand?

Standing for Election; "Seeing plans through"; Bob Middlewood;
Charlie Middlewood; Bob on the attack; Jack Passey; "Cherry" Fawcett

Standing for Election

The next local election was in 1967, and at first it was not in my mind to stand
for election myself, but to help others of like mind. I had been living in Bishop
Auckland for just two and a half years, and few people knew me. There was no
organised Liberal campaign, so I decided to help my friend, journalist Derek
Hebden, to get elected as an Independent in Cockton Hill West. Nominations
closed at noon on the Saturday, and on the Friday evening I was in Derek's
house discussing the election with him and his wife Joan. That day's Evening
Despatch newspaper (now long deceased) printed a list of nominations thus far.
I looked at the nominations for my ward (Cockton Hill East) and found there
were only Conservative and Labour candidates – no Liberals, no Independents.
I complained about this, and Joan Hebden said 'why don't you stand?' So, at
10am sharp the next morning, I was at the Council Offices to collect my
nomination papers. Ten signatures were needed, and by 10.45am I was back at
the Old Bank Chambers with my papers duly completed. I topped the poll and
was elected for this three-seat ward, along with two Tories, ex-police inspector
Charles Middlewood and estate agent Dennis Edkins. One Conservative lost his
seat. Believe it or not, my Nana knew Dennis. She once lived in Grange-over-
Sands and always referred to him as 'the auctioneer's boy'.

"Seeing plans through"

Straight after the election, an old Councillor came knocking on my door. I asked
him in. He congratulated me on my success, and asked if I would support him
as Chairman of the Council. I said I didn't know who else might be standing. So
he tried to sweeten the pill. 'I can tell you a way to make a bit of money,' he said.
The way he described it was this. Each month when the planning list came out,
he would go through it and mark the plans for his own ward. Fair enough. Then
he would go to the people in his ward making the planning applications and ask
them if they would like him to 'see your plans through'. If they said yes, he
would ask for a pound for his "services". Invariably, he would get the pound.
People thought that this would help them get their plans passed, although at that
time urban and rural councils had no planning powers but had to be consulted.
This old Councillor would sit through the Works Committee meeting when the
plans were considered and say nothing. Inevitably, almost every plan was passed

"on the nod". He would then return to his constituents and give them the good news, and they would consider it a pound well spent. Needless to say, I did not take up his suggestion.

It was quite something to be a Councillor in those days. Unlike today, you got a lot of respect, although I'm bound to say that in those days [this is 1967] Councillors were not paid at all and in general received no expenses whatsoever. But of course there were a lot more Councillors then than now, something like four or five times as many, and most councils were much smaller. Bishop Auckland UDC for example had 36 members who had perhaps two or three meetings a month, and always in the evenings. Now the former UDC area is represented by just eight councillors, and even this small number may well be reduced in the near future.

Another early visitor was a very anxious constituent. This gentleman was desperate for me to come round to his house straight away. There was a serious and urgent matter that I needed to look into. I went round to his house, and he took me through to the back and into his back garden. 'There!' he said, pointing to the back of his house. I looked carefully. I couldn't see anything untoward. 'There it is,' he said, 'do you see that downcomer [drain pipe]? My neighbour put that downcomer there, and he's fixed it on my side of the property, not his. It's wrong, it should be moved to his side'. As hard as I looked, I couldn't tell where the boundary lay between the two terraced houses, and whether or not his assertion was true. So I played for time. 'When did he put this downcomer there?" I asked. 'Oh, 14 years ago,' was his reply, so I had my get-out. 'I'm afraid it's past the Statute of Limitations,' I replied in pseudo-legal jargon. But not every constituent was as easy to deal with as that.

On another occasion I was summoned to meet a whole family in their council house. They told me that the Council was riddled with corruption, and they had the evidence to expose it. I asked them what they wanted me to do. 'If we give you the evidence, will you bring it to the Council's attention?' they asked. 'Certainly,' I replied, 'if it's genuine I'll be happy to do just that'. But when I asked to see the evidence, they were reluctant to show me. After further prevarication, it transpired that what they wanted to happen was, at the next full Council meeting, they would hand me an envelope in the Council Chamber, in the middle of the meeting, and I would immediately stand up and read out the letter, sight unseen. So, I made my excuses and left. I asked them to send me the information, but I'm still waiting.

Bob Middlewood

At that time Labour Leader, Alderman Bob Middlewood was the dominant personality on the Council. He had been Chairman of the Council eight or nine times, once every three years – it was a three-year election cycle in those days. Bob ran the Labour Group with an iron fist, brooking no opposition whatsoever. He was a powerful personality and an effective speaker. Like many of his ilk, he would make up policy on the hoof, knowing whichever way he went, his flock would follow, obedient and unquestioning. On several occasions I've seen him giving a speech on these lines: 'This is the most ridiculous proposition ever to come before this Council, I am totally opposed to every word of it,' he would say, with all the fervour of a revivalist preacher. So I could see all the Labour members getting ready to vote against the motion. When Bob paused in his oration (which was never, ever short), some would even start to put up their hands to vote it down. Then Bob would have a Damascus moment. 'On the other hand, this proposition does have some merit, so I suppose we'll have to vote for it. I move in favour'. So immediately all the Labour members would put up their hands in favour of the motion, as instructed by Bob. It was as clear and as simple as that. The Labour members always voted together, and always as Bob told them – always.

I've mentioned that Councillors were not paid then, but there were a few perks. The Council Chairman had a drinks bar in his room, and it was traditional after ever full Council meeting for all Members of the Council, regardless of Party, to join the Chairman for a drink. One particular year when he was Chairman, I think for the last time, Bob kept the Chairman's room locked. There were no free drinks after meetings. In retaliation, the Labour members boycotted Bob's Civic Ball. But Bob had the last laugh. Come the next AGM, which followed the three-yearly local elections, the Council was evenly split eighteen-eighteen between Labour and non-Labour. As the retiring Chairman – although no longer a Councillor – Bob would have taken the chair at the start of the meeting. His casting vote for a new Chairman would have put Labour in power. But Bob wasn't there – he deliberately went on a sea cruise. The non-Labour Vice Chairman took the chair, Labour failed to get the casting vote, and they remained in opposition.

There were lots of tales about Bob, who certainly sailed close to the wind on a number of occasions. For example, it was said he would be drinking after hours in the Wear Valley Hotel in Bishop Auckland when there would be a phone call. There was going to be a police raid. It would have been sensational for the Chairman of the Police Authority (Bob) to be caught drinking after hours, so he was given the tip-off and got out of the pub, leaving others to their fate. It was said that many of the materials used in building Bob's new bungalow came from the Council depot, delivered by Council wagon. But when people told these stories, it wasn't with envy, it was with admiration. Bob was doing something clever and getting away with it. He was a local boy made good - that's what people liked.

Certainly Bob had a big ego. Jack Passey, the Council Clerk, told me of what used to happen when Bob was away at a conference. Each day a large brown envelope bearing the Council crest would be sent, addressed to Bob at his hotel. Bob would be sitting in the hotel lounge when a flunky would come through waving this large brown envelope (which had nothing whatsoever inside) calling out 'Colonel Middlewood, Colonel Middlewood, package for Colonel Middlewood'. Bob was indeed a Colonel and a Deputy Lord Lieutenant, and that was his title. So Bob would stand up, wave and shout 'Colonel Middlewood here', ensuring he was both seen and heard by the assembled gathering, to receive his empty envelope. But we all have egos, and Bob had good reason to feel good about himself. As he was apt to tell you, he had come from very poor beginnings, 'when the seat of my pants was hanging out'. Bob had a brother Charles, who was a Tory councillor. The two brothers seemed to me to be as different as chalk and cheese, but they were both strong characters with distinct personalities.

Charlie Middlewood

In my first election in 1967, Charles and I were both elected for the Cockton Hill East ward, as it was then. Charles didn't like my intervention, and called me a Communist, despite the fact that I was an active member of the Liberal Party. From his perspective, I was a newcomer, a long-haired radical student type who must therefore obviously be a Communist. The truth was that as a student I had campaigned vigorously against the Communists of various sorts who tended to dominate student politics at the time. The Communists employed some underhand tactics. For example, when I was elected as one of the college representatives to the National Union of Students, they made sure that someone else went in my place by the simple expedient of going mob-handed to Newcastle Central Station and physically preventing me from boarding the train to go to an NUS meeting. They tried to kick me out of meetings by invoking obscure procedural rules, but I knew the rules better than they did. I was also "barred out" of the Union building at one time, for daring to expose the fact that half the takings in Rag Week went on "expenses". Student politics was vicious, tough, unprincipled and uncompromising – excellent training for being a local Councillor.

27

Bob on the attack

The Council Chamber in Bishop Auckland Town Hall was small and intimate, with tiered seating. This made for some exciting and passionate debates, as the Members were squashed in check-by-jowl. As I recall, there was just one row of seats for the public, and the press bench was only a few feet away from the Members. This enabled "Uncle Bob" to vent his wrath on a very young journalist, Mike Amos, sitting close by. At that time Amos wrote a column called "the Words of Amos", which Bob quickly turned into "the words that shame us". As for me, Bob dismissed me comprehensively at my very first Council meeting. According to Bob, I was an incomer, a liar and a worthless individual [shades of John Richardson to come!]. The fact that he singled me out in his first speech at my first Council meeting - before I had even said a word - was in fact a peculiar sort of compliment. With his excellent political nous, Bob recognised that I was a danger to the Labour hegemony, and he was absolutely right. Bob Middlewood was a powerful man, an effective speaker and a superb political operator, no doubt about that. But all he was interested in was his own power and prestige, nothing more.

Jack Passey

The real power on Bishop Auckland UDC was exercised, mainly behind the scenes, by the Council Clerk, John (Jack) Passey. I liked Mr Passey a lot. He seemed to me to be a man who was not only totally in command of his job, but was absolutely dedicated to it. He was also very robust in his dealings with the Members of the Council. On one occasion I recall him saying: 'what you people should do is to meet once a year and make all your decisions for the next twelve months. Tell us what you want, don't bother us anymore, and come back in a year's time. If we haven't done what you want, then you can kick our backsides'. Whenever there was a problem, Jack Passey had a solution. At one time, when quite a number of Members were returned unopposed at elections, it seemed to be the practice – before my time – that the sitting Councillors would be automatically re-elected. Apparently this transpired on one occasion in St. Helens, a two-member ward. The two sitting Labour members had been returned unopposed in previous elections, so this time they didn't bother to put in any nomination forms. But on this one occasion, an Independent candidate decided to stand and was therefore elected unopposed, leaving one vacancy. One of the Labour men had to lose his seat, but they couldn't decide which one. They had both come onto the Council at the same time, so there was no question of seniority. Jack called the two men into his office. They couldn't agree who would stand down, so Jack read the Riot Act. If they didn't play ball, he would call a by-election, and they would have to take their chances, perhaps with another Independent candidate. Jack said: 'you two go outside, I don't care what

28

you do, toss a coin or whatever, but only one of you is to come back in'. And so it was done. The two men went outside, tossed a coin, and the winner was co-opted back onto the Council.

Jack Passey laid down the law to all the Councillors, including me. After my first election victory, I was full of the enthusiasm of youth. For my first Council meeting, I put down no fewer than seven motions. This was far too much for Jack, and he called me in. 'You can have three items on the agenda and no more,' was his ruling, which needless to say I had to accept. Mr Passey's wife was French-Canadian, very exotic. She was much involved in the town twinning with our French counterparts in Ivry-sur-Seine near Paris. The trouble was, it was said, she spoke French with a strong Canadian accent, so she wasn't always understood. The other thing I was told about her was that she was a very poor driver. The Passeys lived in Newlands Avenue, just off Cockton Hill Road, and Mrs Passey had the reputation of taking the corner very sharply, so if you were crossing over to Cockton Hill Club, you had to watch yourself to make sure she didn't come flying round.

"Cherry" Fawcett
When I was first elected to Bishop Auckland UDC in 1967, there was one other Liberal on the council, Harold "Cherry" Fawcett. Cherry lived in Cockton Hill but was a Councillor for the Town ward. For six successive elections - that's 18 years – Cherry's election technique was always the same. On polling day, he would stand on the corner by the main polling station at St Peter's Church and greet the public on their way to vote. Cherry was very popular, a well-known figure in the town, and this tactic was obviously effective. This was proven when, at his seventh election in 1970, Cherry decided it was safe for him to go on holiday at election time, and so he was absent on voting day. He lost his seat. I guess that when people went to vote and saw that Cherry was not standing in his usual place, they assumed he wasn't standing in the election. That left me as the only Liberal on the Council. Two years later Cherry regained his seat on the Council, joining me in Cockton Hill. It was then I found out that Cherry never did any "case work", the almost daily requests that Councillors get from their constituents on just about any subject you care to mention. I once asked Cherry what he did when people called at his door with a problem. 'I refer them to the appropriate Department of the Council' was his answer. But Cherry was hugely popular and would always get 150-200 votes more than me when we were elected together.

Chapter Six

Olive: Tales of Tommy Hall

"How do you say Charlerois?"; "Sunderland have scored!";
"There's something wrong with me water!"; Disappearing pens;
"Who's going to pay for th'electric?"; "Tommy Turkenkoffer";
Tommy gets the sack

"How do you say Charlerois?"

What had been the Estates & Property Committee became the Technical Committee, and I became Vice Chairman with the redoubtable Roddymoor councillor Tommy Hall as Chairman. For all Tommy's eccentricities, he was a good man and what he didn't know about politics wasn't worth knowing. Another of my interests was town twinning. Bishop Auckland already had a twinning arrangement with French town Ivry-sur-Seine, so it was decided that we should look for another town for Wear Valley to twin with. We get a letter from Charlerois in Belgium and this came to the Technical Committee for consideration. The Committee Chairman, Cllr Tommy Hall came to me with the letter and asked me how to pronounce the name of this Belgian town that wanted to twin with us. I said 'Charlerois' (Sharlawah) in the correct way, and as Tommy walked up to take his place in the chair, he was saying 'Sharlawah, Sharlawah, Sharlawah, Sharlawah'. The meeting got under way and when it came to that item, Tommy said: 'We've had a letter from this town in Belgium called, um, er, Charlie Roy'. Tommy realized he had got it wrong and blurted out: 'Oh God, Olive, I've made a mistake haven't I?' So I had to give the correct pronunciation. Unfortunately, Charlerois got involved in their own local government reorganization, so that twinning arrangement didn't come off. We had to look elsewhere and eventually linked up with Bad Oeynhausen in Germany. Being involved with Belgium a lot over the years, I still have a good laugh about it whenever Charlerois is mentioned.

"Sunderland have scored!"

Tommy Hall didn't bother overmuch about details of policy or indeed about policy atall – he left all that to the Leader "JR" (John Richardson). Tommy was apt to get bored when policy issues were discussed at any length, and during these long and boring meetings he had a habit of listening to soccer commentary on his little transistor radio, using a plug and an earpiece so as not to disturb the proceedings. On one such occasion, a high-ranking Party official came to speak to the Labour Group in Crook. It so happened that Sunderland had a game on at the same time. Knowing Tommy's habits, JR commissioned me to keep a close

30

eye on the King of Roddymoor to make sure he behaved himself. JR took the chair and introduced the speaker.

"Sunderland have scored!"

During the speaker's discourse, JR kept looking at Tommy and back at me, obviously bothered about Tommy and what he might be doing. I kept looking over at Tommy as well, but the ear he used for his earpiece was on the opposite side to me and I couldn't see if he had it in or not. Nor could I get up and walk round the back of the Council Chamber and look at the other side of Tommy's head! Just as the speaker was in the middle of a rousing call for action, both of Tommy's hands shot up in the air. 'Sunderland have scored!' he yelled, at the top of his voice. The speaker halted in mid-oration, looked bemused, all our members tried not to laugh, and JR gave Tommy the blackest of black looks. But JR couldn't say anything, and the speaker recovered his composure and resumed his speech. Fortunately there were no more goals, at least until after the meeting had finished. Afterwards, JR, still fuming, admonished an unrepentant Tommy – but in vain. 'Why should I listen to that beggar when there's a match on?' was his explanation, logical to Tommy if to no-one else.

"There's something wrong with me water!"

Tommy Hall often got the wrong end of the stick. On one occasion when he rang me, the conversation went something like this: Tommy - 'I've had this wife on the phone. She said can you help me? I'm having trouble with me water, it's all brown and smells horrible. So I telt her, it's the doctor thoo wants to see, missus, not me. She said, it's not that that's wrong with me, you daft beggar, it's me tap water that's all brown and horrible. So I said I would make enquiries. Have you got the Water Board's number, Olive?" But I couldn't answer him, I was laughing that much it hurt.

"Who's going to pay for th'electric?"

Tommy Hall was chairman of the Technical Committee. At one meeting, the Crook by-pass was being discussed. Tommy asked – quite sensibly – if there was going to be any street lighting. On being told 'No, but there will be cats' eyes in the middle of the road', Tommy expostulated: 'they're all very well, these cats' eyes, but who's going to pay for th'electric?'

Disappearing pens

That leads me to another amusing incident which involved, inevitably, Cllr Tommy Hall. Tommy, Cllr Richardson (JR) and myself went to London for a seminar in organized by the BBC. It's common practice at these sort of events for the host organization to hand out pens and other material advertising themselves. I happened to be standing by the doorway of the seminar room as this little man from the BBC was putting pens and notepads onto each of the seats. Then I saw Tommy Hall sneaking into the room. Wondering what he was up to, I peeped through the door and there was Tommy, collecting up all of these pens from all of the seats. That was typical of Tommy. Although not short of a bob or two, he just couldn't resist anything that was free and whatever was going, he would help himself to the full, whether he needed them or not. When he was staying in an hotel, he would take away all the little soaps and shampoo sachets. On this occasion, taking all the pens – before the seminar had even started – was going a bit too far, even for Tommy. So I went to JR and told him what I had seen. John Richardson was adamant. 'Tell him to put them all back,' he ordered, and I passed this instruction on to Tommy.

Just as we returned to the seminar room, the little BBC man also came back in. He looked around the room, and his face was a picture. All the pens had gone! It was obvious he was thinking: 'I'm sure I put pens out on all the seats, I'm positive'. So he just shook his head and went out. Tommy and I went round and put all the pens back again. Back came the little BBC man with a whole load more pens. When he looked round the room and saw all the pens back again, his face was even more of a picture than it was before. He shook his head sadly and slowly went away, no doubt thinking he must be going mad! I said to Tommy: 'Don't you ever do that again in a place like this. It's absolutely ridiculous'. John Richardson also took Tommy to task. 'You are the Deputy Leader and you shouldn't be doing things like that'. Later we did have a good laugh about it because I thought 'well, Thomas, for once we've topped you!'

"Tommy Turkenkoffer"

Often Tommy would give us a good laugh without him realizing it. Tommy used to carry his things around in a battered old shopping bag, even at official functions. On one occasion in Germany he had the small gifts we give from one Council to another in this old shopping bag. When it was time for him to go up to the front and make the presentations, up he went with these things in his old, battered bag. The Germans, who have a lot of Turkish gastarbeiters (= guest workers, ie immigrant workers) living in their country, started to whisper "Tommy Turkenkoffer". Turkenkoffer in German means "Turkish Suitcase", a reference to the unlicensed street vendors who used to sell goods and trinkets from their old suitcases. It was said that when Tommy made speeches on these occasions, they had to be translated twice – once into English and then into German.

"Tommy Turkenkoffer"

Tommy gets the sack

You couldn't help liking Tommy, and on one particular occasion we all felt extremely sorry for him, when he was sacked as Deputy Leader. After years of blind loyalty to JR, Tommy was finally pushed too far at the Labour Group Meeting and called JR a "dictator". He was finished from

33

that moment on. *[Chris: I was in the Members' Room just before the following Council Meeting, when the Chief Executive Alan Dobson came in and spoke to Tommy, who was no more than two feet away from me].* 'Councillor Hall, let me show you where you're going to be sitting from now on,' said Dobson, who took Tommy by the arm and led him into the Council Chamber. A shell-shocked Tommy was shown to his new seat on the back benches, and when the meeting started, a new Deputy Leader was sitting next to JR. It was a simple as that. JR's word was law, and anyone who crossed him had to take the consequences.

Chapter Seven

Chris: Chairman of Works

I get Harold's job; First "Joint Use" Scheme; South Church Industrial Estate;
First Liberal Group; Double Act; Betty Todd

I get Harold's job

After three years on the Council, I became Chairman of the grandly-named
Works, Estates & Property committee, the same position that Harold Stephenson
had held when he decided that I should be appointed as Senior Assistant
Engineer with the Council. I'd like to think that I did a good job in my role as
Works Committee Chairman. One of the schemes that I followed up with great
enthusiasm did not come to full fruition, but through no fault of mine. The
government was planning to bring in what became known as GIAs – General
Improvement Areas. This was a system of government grants to local councils
to improve the environment. I seized this opportunity with both hands. Even
before the legislation had been passed, on my instructions we prepared the
groundwork. In total, Bishop Auckland UDC had no fewer than thirty-three
GIAs, giving every town and village in the district a chance of renewal, and we
were ready on day one. This rush of enthusiasm shocked the mandarins of
Whitehall. One small District Council asking for 33 GIAs – ridiculous! We
argued that, within the legislation, there was no limit to the number of schemes
we could have, but to no avail. The powers-that-be in Whitehall allowed us to
have only three GIAs, so 30 areas were disappointed – this after we had put huge
efforts into informing and consulting every one of our 33 local communities.

This had the unfortunate knock-on effect of making a lot of people
disillusioned. In each case we had gone through a consultation exercise with the
local people to plan what was best for each area, very democratic and also very
necessary. So a lot of people's hopes were raised - and dashed. The alternative
would have been to put forward only a handful of plans in the first place, but that
too would have caused problems. The basic fact of the situation is that, time
after time, government comes up with a super wheeze whereby they make some
headline-grabbing announcement, only to find that the response is greater than
they thought it would be. Funding is limited, and so the whole thing has to be
cut back. Invariably, it's the local Council and indeed the local Councillors who
get the blame, not the government. In later years exactly the same thing
happened with Estate Action, a scheme to improve run-down council housing
estates. We had quite a lot of these estates in Wear Valley, but having to start late
– for reasons of party politics – we were only able to get one off the ground, and

that at a reduced grant. But one was better than none.

First "Joint Use" Scheme

One project I look back on with much pride is the "joint use" scheme at the King James I Comprehensive School in Bishop Auckland. Although it had long been a policy of mine that school premises should be used for the community as well as for children's education, this was the first such scheme in County Durham. Why Bishop Auckland was picked, I have no idea, but again I grabbed the opportunity with both hands. My colleagues on the urban council did take some persuading that this was a worthwhile project, but in the end they backed it. The idea was that the District Council would put money into additional facilities on the school site for community use as well as the school. Both school and community would benefit, and so it proved. An indoor bowling centre was built, along with a lounge that could be used by visitors as well as staff and pupils. At the same time, a Community Association was started and for fourteen years I was very actively involved in it, most of that time either as Chairman or Vice-Chairman. The Community Association provided a huge range of activities for people of all ages, and is thriving still.

South Church Industrial Estate

Another project I was able to get the Council to agree with was the setting-up of the South Church Industrial Estate, another joint enterprise between the District and County councils. Although its implementation was delayed due to another bout of petty political decision-making, when JR (John Richardson) came into office as Leader of Wear Valley Council, it was too late for him to prevent it going ahead, although he did try. The South Church Enterprise Park, as it now is, has provided hundreds of jobs over the years for local people and I count it as a great success. When JR took control of the new Wear Valley Council in 1974 he didn't just put the brakes on the South Church Industrial Estate, he put the brakes on development at Bishop Auckland in general. Likewise, nothing was done about the town centre redevelopment, despite the fact that when I was Chairman of Works at Bishop Auckland UDC, we had signed a contract with a firm of developers to create a new town centre. Absolutely nothing was done about this for two years, 1974-76. When in 1976 I first became Leader of the Council, I realised that something had to be done or Bishop Auckland would be left behind as a shopping centre. We also go the South Church Industrial Estate under way at last.

First Liberal Group

Cherry Fawcett regained his seat on the Council in a by-election in 1972, and it was then with another Councillor we formed the first Liberal Group. We also reformed the Bishop Auckland constituency party, with me as Chairman. This did not sit well with Cherry, who thought he should have been Chairman. As nice as he was, if Cherry had been chairman, nothing would have happened. Cherry's idea of being a chairman was to sit in the chair and conduct meetings, something he could do superbly well, but that was it. The campaigning work to recruit new members, organise election campaigns and build up the Party fell to me. Our newly-formed local Party was a very small band. I think there were just five of us at the first meeting: me, Cherry and the other Liberal Councillor, Tommy Dixon from Eldon Lane and Betty Hardisty, wife of local soccer hero Bobby Hardisty. Tommy, whose mother had been a stalwart Liberal, later became a Councillor.

Double Act

However, Cherry's chairmanship skills did stand us in good stead later on Wear Valley Council. At one meeting of the full Council, with Cherry in the chair, I counted up (as I always did) and found we were in a minority. Labour members were always better at turning up for meetings. Cherry too had spotted that we

"A dab hand with the gavel"

were in the minority, and he gave me a nod and a wink. We then did our well-practised double act. As Council Leader, I would propose adoption of each minute in turn, Cherry would say 'Agreed?', pause for just a second, then clash down his Chairman's gavel with a firm 'Agreed!'. We were half-way through the meeting when our Labour friends realised what was going on. Everything else on the agenda was 'referred back for further consideration' as Labour exercised its majority of the day, negating everything remaining on the agenda even if they agreed with it. Needless to say, we brought everything back again to the next

37

meeting, making sure all our members were there, and passed everything through. I don't often enjoy this type of "fun and games", as I regard them as a distraction and a waste of time, but I did enjoy this one.

Betty Todd

Another of our very earliest members was Betty Todd, who has been a constant tower of strength for the Party throughout the years. She stood many times before finally being elected as a Councillor in 1991. Betty was Leader of the Council for one year, and it was enormously pleasing for me and many others when she was elected as the last Chairman of Wear Valley Council, 2008/09. If anyone deserves a medal, Betty does. Other members who joined our little band early on included Melvin Bradley, Doreen McMahon, Norma Ainscough and Leo Gillett from Coundon, Jean Cook from Bishop Auckland and Tom and Joan Lauder from Crook. None of these became Councillors (Tom had been on Crook & Willington UDC) but they helped pave the way for others.

Chapter Eight

Olive: First Lady Chairman

*Thrilled & Honoured; JR steps in; I ruin a cream cake; Staying sober;
Citizen of Honour; Olive the Chanteuse; A Chairman's highs and lows;
Queen's Garden Party*

Thrilled & Honoured

In 1980 Tommy Hall became Chairman of the Council and I was Council Vice Chairman. I was over the moon at the prospect of being Chairman of this new council. Several other people also wanted the position, but I felt I had worked hard and had earned it. I was also very pleased that Tommy was Council Chairman, because I knew I could learn a lot from him. I went to functions in Bishop Auckland, Weardale, Crook, Willington and Tow Law. It grounded me for the Chairman's job to follow the next year. I was really thrilled and highly honoured when in May 1981 I became the first lady Chairman of the new authority. We have had several lady Chairmen of Wear Valley since then, all I am proud and pleased to say have got there on their merits and not on anything else.

JR steps in

There was an older, lady Councillor who would have loved to have been the first woman Chairman of Wear Valley. I'd had problems with this lady in the past, and I wasn't surprised at all at something that happened on the day I was due to be made Chairman, which is akin to a Mayor-making ceremony. A Council Chairman or Mayor have exactly the same duties and responsibilities, by the way. This lady councillor told the Leader of the Council, Cllr John Richardson, that she was not very well and wanted him to take her home – straight away – meaning she and John would miss the ceremony. Now John Richardson is a very shrewd character. He knew the problems that existed between this lady and myself, and he said: 'No, I'm terribly sorry, I can't take you home now but I will take you home after Olive's been made Chairman. I'm the Leader of the Council and it's my duty to see Olive become Chairman'. So this lady had to sit and watch me become Chairman and I could see that it didn't go down very well with her. However, I went to her after the meeting and said: 'Look, you know I am very proud and very privileged as you would have been to be Chairman of the Council'. We sort of patched things up after that, but I was eternally grateful to John Richardson for doing that. He is a very experienced politician and he really went up in my estimation that day.

I ruin a cream cake

My first official duty as Council Chairman was a small function in Crook. Afterwards there was a buffet and I forgot about having this big chain of office on my person. The centre-piece of the spread was a beautiful cream cake. I leaned forward and said: 'Oh, doesn't that look lovely!' and of course the medallion went straight through this lovely cream cake. I felt absolutely awful, the medallion was covered in cream and everybody laughed. But it broke the ice

Licking it clean

for me and taught me always to watch what you are doing at these official functions. You tend to forget that you are wearing a big chain with a heavy medallion on the end of it. I enjoyed going to functions all over the District. I met up with a lot of my friends in Weardale and Tow Law, and obviously in Crook and Willington. But I made a conscious effort to go to functions in Bishop Auckland whenever possible. I was already a member of the Bishop Auckland twinning association. Speaking fluent French, I often found myself translating from English to French and vice versa. At the Council's annual Civic Ball, we always invited guests from our French twin town Ivry-sur-Seine, and I visited there also. It meant that I couldn't enjoy myself because I was often "on duty" and had to listen very carefully to what was being said and then translating. It was very difficult sometimes, especially when Tommy Hall spoke in his Durham dialect.

Staying sober

Ivry Council had a Communist majority and a Mayor, Jacque Laloe. M Laloe was a directly-elected Mayor, a powerful man, who was also a Communist. As I recall, he was elected for a seven-year term, so he was very relaxed and not worrying about the next election all the time, as we are apt to do in this country. Although Ivry was a small town just outside Paris, the Council ran all the local services including the local hospital. Once, I asked the Mayor, 'M Laloe, how do you always appear to be sober when you drink a lot of wine? It doesn't seem to go to your head.'. 'Ah,' he said, 'Olive, I will give you a tip. It ruins the wine but it will keep you from feeling heavy or getting drunk quickly. You see this bottle of water here?' The Mayor put a small amount of wine into his glass, filled it up with water, and carried on like that for the rest of the evening. Everybody thought he was drinking a lot of wine, but in fact most of it was water. Ever since then, if I have to go to a function and wine is on the menu, I always add water to my wine. So if I have several glasses, it dousn't make much difference. This is a very good tip, which I have since passed it on to many chairmen and others. I'm not a big drinker and it's easy to get carried away.

Citizen of Honour

It was my luck to be Council Chairman on the twentieth anniversary of the twinning of Bishop Auckland and Ivry, now between Wear Valley and Ivry. It fell to the Liberal-Independent administration in power 1976-79 to decide on a twin town for Wear Valley, in addition to the Ivry link which was continuing. Liberal Leader Chris Wood from Bishop Auckland and Independent Cllr Jimmy Smith from Willington exchanged visits with German spa town Bad Oeynhausen in North-Rhine Westphalia and it was Jimmy as Wear Valley Council Chairman on 18th June 1977 who signed the Partnerschaft agreement. Bad Oeynhausen is a beautiful place. I've been there many times and have many friends over there. So we were invited to Ivry for this 20th anniversary, and one evening there was a function, but exactly what about I didn't know. They had forgotten that I could speak French, and I overheard a conversation and my name was mentioned. I thought: 'My God, what's this?' so I picked up a programme and saw they were going to make Cllr Mrs Olive Brown a Citizen of Honour of Ivry. Not knowing about this, obviously I hadn't written a speech. I did thank them for the honour, but not as well as if I had been prepared.

The local French Member of Parliament George Gosnett was there, as was the British Ambassador – a lady. Because Ivry had links with Czechoslovakia, there was an Ambassador from Czechoslovakia, as well as ambassadors from Germany and Russia. I got the Key to the Town of Ivry, a sash and a written statement which has adorned my wall at home ever since. It was a fantastic and wonderful experience. I felt absolutely marvellous and very honoured, because I love to speak French and I love the French people very much. I thought this was the ultimate honour in my life. I was thrilled to bits when the British Ambassador came over and said; 'Mrs Brown, you speak wonderful French. Have you ever thought of joining the Diplomatic Corps?' and I thought, well, I wish I had. She was very nice and said 'you did that wonderfully well'. The other Ambassadors came and they all said I spoke very good French, and how unusual it was for English people to speak another language. So when I told then I spoke German as well, they said 'well done!' I was pleased to be received like that and also thrilled. I was just walking on air for the rest of the night.

That was an apt remark by the British Ambassador, as I might well have had a career in the Foreign Service and, who knows? I might have become an Ambassador myself. I was still in my teens when I applied for a job in the Foreign Office in London. I was good at languages, I was very interested in the wider world and I wanted to travel. So I went down to London where I took an exam and had an interview. All that went well, I passed the exam and had a good interview. But one afternoon I happened to be standing on the forecourt of Charing Cross station, close by Trafalgar Square. It was the rush hour, and all I could see around me were swarms and swarms of people, hundreds, even thousands it seemed, everybody hurrying here and there. It appeared to me to be a scene of sheer madness, and I just didn't like it. So I withdrew my application and came back to Crook, where indeed I have been very happy ever since. But a tiny part of me still can't help imagining what might have been but for the rush hour and the roar of London traffic

Olive the Chanteuse

There's a French song, a favourite of mine, that the Ivry people know I like very much: "J'Attendrai" by Dalida, and they asked me to sing it in French. I'm not much of a singer but I did sing it in French and they thought it was lovely. Another favourite song of mine is "Je ne regrette rien" by Edith Piaf, and I sang that as well. It made my evening. Everybody has heard of Edith Piaf, but Dalida is not so well known, despite her hugely successful international singing career. She was born Yolande Christina Gigliotti in Egypt – her parents were Italian immigrants. She wanted to be an actress and her first big break was becoming Miss Egypt. She appeared in an Egyptian film with Omar Sharif and moved to

Paris to boost her acting career, but found fame as a singer after changing her name to Dalida. She recorded in several languages, mainly French, and her records sold in the millions – 86 million in all - even one year topping Piaf.

Olive sings in French

Dalida became the biggest-selling female singer in Italy where she was made an honorary citizen. J'Attendrai (I will wait for you) was the first disco record made in France, and it has always been a favourite of mine. Dalida had a tumultuous private life and sadly committed suicide in 1987 at the age of 54.

A Chairman's highs and lows

A dreadful incident occurred during my Chairmanship in 1982. Detective Police Constable James Porter was shot dead after an armed robbery in Bishop Auckland. I arranged to have a collection for DC Porter's family and we raised a tremendous amount of money. I got donations from all over because it was quite unheard of in those days for something like this to happen in a 'a small sleepy market town' as Bishop was called in the press. The highlight of every Chairman's year is the Civic Ball. Local MP Ernest Armstrong asked me who I would like to have as the guest speaker. I had a great of admiration for Labour MP Denis Healey who was at that time Deputy Leader of the Party, so I asked for him. Ernest Armstrong came back and said that Denis would be delighted to come. I was over the moon, and so Denis Healey came to my civic ball along with his charming wife Edna. We had an absolutely wonderful evening. Everything went like clockwork. Of course Denis Healey was excellent and made a very good speech which everybody enjoyed. As well as Councillors and their families and civic heads from other authorities, there were business people and others prominent in the community. There were also friends that you hadn't seen for a long time, and perhaps some you who were at school with you. You would always say they hadn't changed, even if they had.

Queen's Garden Party

Every Council Chairman gets the chance to go to Buckingham Palace for the Queen's Garden Party. This I particularly enjoyed, never thinking that a good few years later I would be going to Buckingham Palace again for something else(!) So Ken and I made the most of our visit to Buckingham Palace. It was a really wonderful day, the sun shone and we did enjoy it. The only thing I didn't enjoy was having to wear a hat, something I have never done because I don't like hats, but it was a great day nonetheless. On another occasion, I was invited to go to Speaker's House in Westminster by the Rt Hon George Thomas MP, Speaker of the House of Commons, for a dinner. This was again most enjoyable, and I met a lot of interesting people. During my years as Chairman, the Council decided to have a Wear Valley Marathon. Thora Hird and Bill Fraser were filming a series in Weardale. They agree to come and set off the run. Bill Fraser couldn't stay, but Thora Hird was here for most of the day. She was a wonderful lady. It was ironic that the winner that day was Max Coleby, because a few years later he became manager of Sport & Leisure at Wear Valley. *[Chris: there were four Wear Valley Marathons, and I ran in all four, plus several half marathons, 10K races and triathlons, all organised by WVDC].*

Chapter Nine

Chris: Wear Valley is formed

Shadow Council; "National Party" candidates; Come and join us!;
Blessed are the Peacemakers; Town centre redevelopment; "Shelf rents";
John Callaghan; Mary Tarren; "Peggy" Preshous

Shadow Council

The first elections to the newly-formed Wear Valley District Council were held in 1973, giving the Members a "shadow year" before the new Council took over on 1st April 1974. It just had to be April Fools' Day, didn't it? Anyhow, that election saw Labour gain a narrow majority with 21 members, including Cllrs Olive Brown and Don White who were taken on board despite defeating official Labour candidates in their wards, and Reg Spark from Stanhope who was a Labour member but somehow always forgot to put "Labour" on his nomination form. There were 11 Independents and nine Liberals. The fact of the matter is that JR (Labour Leader John Richardson) ran rings round the Independents who were mainly from Weardale where the Rural District Council had always been non-political. By the time the Independents woke up to what was going on, it was too late and JR was firmly entrenched in power. This was a culture shock for the well-meaning but politically naïve Independents who readily joined with us Liberals to take control after the next election in 1976.

"National Party" candidates

When the nominations were published for the 1973 district council elections, there was something of a stir in the national press. Party political allegiance was listed on the ballot papers for the first time. Many candidates misunderstood what this was for, and put down their occupation instead. So we had a lot of people apparently standing for the "Housewife" Party, the "Publican" Party, the "Estate Agent" Party, the "Works Manager" Party, the "Typist" Party, and of course there were many candidates standing for the "Retired" Party. Our friends up the Dale decided they would declare their allegiance as "No Party". Fair enough, but all they put in the "Party" column was NP, ie No Party. Political editors of several national newspapers sent their hacks up to the wilds of Weardale, looking for this unexpectedly large group of candidates apparently standing for the National Party, which was the main Fascist-type Party in the UK at the time. They were disappointed, and returned to London without a story, but waxing lyrical about friendly Dales hospitality and wonderful Weardale teas.

Come and join us!

We would have done better in the 1973 elections if we had put up more candidates. I learned my lesson, and at every election since then I have put a huge amount of time and energy into fighting as many seats as possible. This paid dividends in the 1976 elections. Although we had a nett gain of just two seats, with the Tories also gaining two seats it was enough to put Labour out of power. Result: Labour 17, Liberals 11, Independents 11, Tories 2. I became Chairman and Leader of the Council, with Independent Jimmy Smith from Sunnybrow as Vice Chairman. Yet we could have taken control in 1973, not just by putting up more candidates, but also if Olive Brown had been one of our candidates – as she might well have been. Olive's recollection is different from mine, but this is how I remember it.

Tom Lauder, an Independent councillor from Crook who had recently joined the Liberal Party, arranged a meeting with him, me and Olive at his house. Olive had been deselected as a Labour candidate and had made up her mind to stand anyway. We talked, and afterwards I drove Olive home as she showed me around her ward in Crook. I was mightily impressed with Olive, both for her considerable personal qualities and her commitment to the people of Crook. Naturally I was keen to have Olive as a Liberal candidate, although there is no doubt she would have been elected no matter what label she had. There was only one problem – we already had a candidate for the Crook East ward.

Now it would have been the easiest thing in the world for me to remove our existing (and admittedly rather weak) candidate and put Olive in her place. That would have been the correct "political" decision. But I have strong moral values and I decided to do what was right rather than what was expedient. So I said: "Sorry, Olive, we would love to have you as a Liberal candidate, but it would have to be for another ward – we already have a candidate for this ward". But for Olive, it had to be that particular ward and nowhere else. So we both stuck by our principles, Olive was duly elected and, with Don White who also defeated an official Labour candidate at Hunwick, was accepted back into the Labour ranks to give JR the two seats he needed to get a majority on the Council. If Olive had joined us in 1973, without doubt we would have gained the majority, and JR would never had been in power. Imagine that!

I do disagree with Olive in one other respect: after the election, I did not try to recruit her or Don White to the Liberal Party. As far as I was concerned, they had both rejoined the Labour Party and that was that. I do not believe in trying to get people to "cross the floor", in fact I am strongly opposed to Councillors changing their allegiance mid-term. To me, that is a falsehood and such people are turncoats who have no respect for themselves, for their Party or for the people who voted for them. If a Councillor is determined to change parties, they should first resign their seat and stand again under their new label - that would be the honest thing to do. Not only do such people damage the Party they supposedly gave their allegiance to and which helped get them elected, they damage local government itself and indeed the whole concept of democracy.

Blessed are the Peacemakers

But all that was still to come, some years down the line. Remarkably, the Liberal-Independent majority group I led 1976-79, with the support of the two Conservatives, Cllr George Liddell (a first-class chair of Finance) and Cllr Margaret Hurst (a true friend to me), lasted the full three-year term, despite many predictions that we 'wouldn't last till Christmas'. I believe this was due in large measure to the diplomatic skills of Cllr Jimmy Smith, first my deputy Chairman and then Chairman of the Council. There were many volatile personalities in our Group, both Liberal and Independent, but Jimmy could always find a way of resolving what were invariably clashes of temperament and personality rather than policy which was my main focus. It has often been said that if Jimmy had regained his seat on the Council in 1991, we might well have avoided the troubles we had. As Leader, I put all my energies into formulating and implementing policies I perceived to be the best for the District and its people. I needed a peacemaker by my side and Jimmy fulfilled that role superbly. When Frances and I married in 1977, Jimmy was our best man, but not I hasten to add in his "peacemaking" capacity! (although he was on hand when Frances lost her voice during the ceremony when she was just about to say 'I do' – but that's another story). George Liddell, by the way, along with Cllr Stewart Fairbairn, were both good friends and mentors to me when I was first elected in 1967. Despite my relative youth and inexperience, these two older councillors backed me to be a committee chairman, and I will always be grateful to them for that.

Town centre redevelopment

During JR's rule 1974-76, nothing whatsoever had been done to progress the new Bishop Auckland shopping centre. The first hurdle we had to overcome was the fact that the contract had no determined length. In 1972 it had been assumed that the development would go ahead straight away, but with the oil crisis of 1973, development companies were drawing in their horns. It was 1976, and I instructed that the developers be given an ultimatum: start the project within twelve months, or we would cancel it. Needless to say, the officers said we couldn't do this, but, on my instructions, we did just that. The developers, who were clearly not in a position to start the scheme at that time, grumbled but in the end simply went away, and we were able to advertise for new developers.

Even that had its problems. From 23 initial enquiries, we drew up a short list of four potential developers, and were to interview all four on the same day. Minutes before we were due to meet the first of these, one of the officers came in to tell me that we would not be able to make an appointment as the District Valuer had not been consulted, and his approval was required for any such scheme – more delay. Then when we did appoint a developer and were putting the plans together, again the officers came to me and said it couldn't go ahead because some of the land was in unknown ownership. The Council was to provide the land as its contribution to the development. Fortunately, I had had experience of land purchase in a previous job I had done as a civil engineer, and I was able to tell our officers that we could overcome these problems by issuing a bond. A bond has the effect that, if an unknown owner turns up sometime in the future when the development is complete, there would be money available to pay him or her on proof of ownership. This was done and we were (finally) able to appoint a developer.

"Shelf rents"

So the Newgate Centre finally went ahead, and I challenge anybody to tell me that this has not been a benefit to Bishop Auckland and the District as a whole. As well as providing new shopping facilities and jobs in the town, there was a cash bonus for the District. I led the negotiations for what are known as "shelf rents". Instead of just handing over the land as our contribution, I determined that in return we had to have a piece of the action, as it were. This arrangement gave the Council a nett profit of between £200,000 and £250,000 a year. The agreement ran for around 25 years before it was terminated when Asda developed their new hypermarket on South Church Road, so I reckon the council taxpayers of Wear Valley have benefited by at least five million pounds for that one decision alone. If I had been Leader at the time when Morrisons came to Bishop Auckland, I could have made many more millions for the District and its residents, but we were out of power and the chance – and the money - was lost.

John Callaghan

One of the most dynamic members of our Liberal-Independent majority that ran the Council 1976-79 was John Callaghan, Independent councillor for Coundon Grange and the undoubted leader of the campaign to abolish Category "D". John was a charismatic character, immensely popular in the Dene Valley villages despite being a homosexual. That never bothered me, but John could also be capricious and too often acted in haste. He was the driving force behind CROVAC – County Redevelopment of Villages Action Committee – and the Durham County Housing Association, which bought up and improved houses in Category "D" villages to prevent their demolition. But John also had a political weakness. He believed that he could persuade the Labour Party not only to remove the Category "D" stigma from the villages, but also to redevelop them. He was wrong, but he was always looking to "do a deal" with Labour. This led me to stand against him - and defeat him – in the County elections of 1973 when he was the sitting County Councillor for his ward. John later became Chairman of Housing on Wear Valley Council but resigned as a Councillor over an alleged (and unproven) conflict of interest. He moved to Scotland where he ran a housing scheme, died and was buried there. Many of us, myself included, went to Scotland for his funeral and I have returned to his grave since.

Mary Tarren

Crook councillor Mary Tarren was sincere but misguided. She had stood under various labels before joining our Party and being elected as a Liberal. Prior to that election, she got into the habit of ringing me every night. Her telephone calls were notoriously long and always one-sided – Mary could speak without pausing for an indefinite period. As one councillor said: 'Mary Tarren rang me just as I was going to wash the car. When she wouldn't stop talking, I put the receiver to one side, went out and washed the car. When I came back, I picked up the receiver and Mary was still talking'. But, leading up to election day, Mary was not satisfied with a mere phone call. I had to go and see her in person. So every night for a week or more, there was nothing for it but to go to Mary's house and listen to her frantic monologue. 'If you don't come, I'm going to pull all my candidates out,' she would threaten. The fact that our members standing in Crook were Liberal candidates not Tarren candidates did not occur to her. But I was always anxious to resolve problems and avoid confrontations and "splits", so I went, I listened and around midnight I came home again. I should have known what would happen. Mary got her claws into me and never let go.

Although she was part of the ruling group on the Council and insisted on being a Committee Chairman, Mary often voted with the Labour Party, but never for any obvious reason. Whenever I asked her why she voted with Labour, she denied doing it! So one particular meeting, every time she voted with the Labour opposition, I started to count: "one, two, three, four," and so on. When I got to "seven", Mary was furious. She turned on me, spitting fire. 'I can't remember why I'm voting against you this week!' she snarled, but voted with us for the rest of the meeting. Others also felt the lash of Mary's tongue. She was "sent to Coventry" by the Council staff when she accused them – in general terms – of being "corrupt". From then on, no member of staff would deal with her direct, and all Council matters for Cllr Tarren had to be channelled through the Chairman of the Council. But I don't bear grudges. When Mary died, I went to her funeral. I was the only Councillor there.

"Peggy" Preshous

Mary (Peggy) Preshous was the ideal sort of person to be a local Councillor. She was a retired head teacher, very well respected, very active and straight as a die. But she served only one term as a Liberal councillor and did not stand again. This is why. One day Peggy observed a Council van draw up near her home, drop off a workman and his grass-mower, and drive away. This was around 9am. The man then mowed this open grassed area, taking about an hour. For another two hours he sat on his mower smoking, until at twelve o'clock the van returned to pick him up. Peggy recounted this episode in condemnatory terms at the next meeting of the Technical Committee – big mistake. Labour councillors were on their feet, shouting and bawling and pointing at Peggy: 'disgraceful attack on an innocent workman just doing his job' etc. If only Peggy had come to me, or had spoken to the Chief Technical Officer or the Chairman of the Technical Committee, her complaint would have been acted upon, I am sure. But Peggy was a strong and independent-minded individual. As far as she was concerned, she had spotted a problem and she had every right to bring it up at a Council meeting. Of course she had that right, and of course the Labour members were wrong to give her grief, but it's a question of how to achieve your objective. A quiet word in the right quarter is very often the best way to resolve a problem. Arthur Nye was another fine Liberal councillor who would have been a major influence if he could have continued on the Council. Julienne Hannibel from Tow Law was another excellent Liberal councillor, very hospitable and great fun in company.

Chapter Ten

Olive: Lady Whip

Black Fishnet Stockings; Labour Lady Councillors; JR knew his stuff;
The Pagoda; JR's heart attack; PC Forty-Nine; Fun and games

Black Fishnet Stockings

All too soon my year of office was over and there was a new Chairman, my deputy Cllr Albert Seddon from Willington duly elected as Chairman of the Council. I took a year out and was then elected Labour Group Whip. This was a very busy job, and it was my job to keep order in the Group. Being a lady Group Whip, they asked me if I wanted some black fishnet stockings and a whip. I said certainly not, it's not that sort of job, but some wag did buy me some fishnet stockings and also a whip! I had a good laugh about it and put them away. I say I had to keep order, but I must say my job was made very easy because the Leader of the Council, Cllr John Richardson, himself always kept people in order. He stood for no nonsense from anyone. I learned a lot from John. Watching him in operation at close quarters stood me in good stead for later on when I became Leader myself. I learned what to avoid as well and how to build on things that I thought that needed building on. Part of my job was to look after all of the Councillors when we went to any functions.

Another of my positions was to represent Wear Valley on the Durham branch of the Association of District Councils where all the eight districts in Durham - including Darlington in those days - got together we got together to discuss matters of mutual interest. It was very interesting because we found out what was happening in other districts, and we had meetings with the local MPs including a certain Tony Blair from Sedgefield. We had a good working relationship with all the County Durham MPs. I became Chairman of this organization, and I also got elected onto the national body which met in London. I was on the ADC's Tourism Committee [Chris: as I was later]. We met councillors from all over England, Wales and Scotland – that was before Scotland and Wales got their own governments. Because I was Group Whip, I wasn't chairman of any committee. This meant I could spend a bit of time seeing how the other half of the world lived, and also gaining experience of what other councils did. We were trying to build on the tourist aspect of Weardale, so it was a challenge which I gratefully accepted. I also represented Wear Valley on the North East Councils Association, which included all local authorities, large and small, from the Humber up to the borders of Scotland. I made some very good friends in Hull and also up in the Borders. I become quite well known, so

"Lady Whip"

whenever I went to functions anywhere, everybody knew me.

Labour Lady Councillors
We have always had a good mix of men and women councillors on Wear Valley Council. There have been a good number of women Labour councillors, and no fewer than eight of us have become Chairman of the Council: Olive Brown (1981-82), June Lee (1988-89), Betty Wilson (1989-90), Belle Bousefield (1997-98), Ann Newton (2000-01), Margaret Pinkney (2002-03), Margaret Douthwaite (2003-04), Margaret Jones (2004-05). This shows what an enlightened Council Wear Valley was. We were one of the first Councils to have a woman Leader (Cllr Mrs Olive Brown), and a woman Chief Executive (Mrs Carole Hughes).

In May 1984, Cllr Teresa (Edie) Moralee, one of the longest-serving Labour Councillors on Crook & Willington and Wear Valley Councils, resigned due to ill health. In Crook Labour Party branch, we had an ideal replacement and a good friend of mine, Rita Richardson (no relation to JR!). Rita was a very outspoken girl, a very good Councillor who did a lot for Crook. Rita was a great help to me and Alan Brooksbank in our ward. Rita was deputy chairman of the Planning Committee for a while, a position she really enjoyed. She decided to stand, and in July 1984 she was elected to represent the Crook South ward. Rita was very forthright but fair, and I knew she would make a good councillor. Rita became Deputy Chairman of the Health Committee and then Deputy Chairman of the Planning Committee and did an excellent job in both positions. Unfortunately, Rita lost her seat in the 1991 elections and decided not to stand again after that. This was the Council's loss because I know she would have gone on to do higher things on the Council.

Another councillor and close friend I served with was Belle Bousfield. She played a great role when I was Leader of the Council and I will pay tribute to her later. Betty Wilson from Stanley was another good Councillor, and there were others, too numerous to mention. We had a good team in those days. I have never been a stick-in-the-mud or head-in-the sand person. I was all for reforming the Labour Party because I felt certain things weren't right. June Lee was elected for the Woodhouse Close Ward in Bishop Auckland in 1995, she was Council Chairman 1988-89, and is still a serving Councillor. During June's term of office as Chairman, the Durham Light Infantry was awarded the Freedom of Bishop Auckland. June was the first Chairman of the Council's Scrutiny Committee and has continued to do a splendid job in this role. She has also been Secretary of the WVDC Labour Group. June has now been elected to the new Durham County unitary authority.

Of course there have been a good number of men who served on WVDC. Over the years I have had the privilege of serving with many good local Councillors. I was in the Crook East ward with Cllr Alan Brooksbank who was a colleague of mine for a long time before he was knocked off the Council in our great defeat of 1991. I have already mentioned Roddymoor councillor Tommy Hall. He was a real character, and he did know a lot about local government. Tommy certainly wasn't politically correct and I don't know what would have happened to him if he'd still been around in recent years. All Tommy cared about was the town he lived in and the people who he represented in his own individual way.

JR knew his stuff

Cllr John Richardson, the first Labour Leader of WVDC, in my estimation is a very good politician. He is an excellent public speaker and he did know his stuff. JR was a very powerful man, one of the old-fashioned Leaders – all powerful - and he did not suffer fools gladly. I must say I learned a lot from "JR" as he was universally known. JR was merciless with people who crossed him, and political opponents like Chris Foote Wood certainly had the full blast of his ire. JR was dictatorial, yet on occasions – when I as Party Whip or his deputy Tommy Hall opposed him – after a fiery discussion, he would see reason. JR led the Council from its formation as a shadow authority in 1973 to 1976, and again from 1979 to 1991 – fifteen years in all.

All leaders, myself included, do have their faults. John Richardson was a really hard man to crack and was very dictatorial in his dealings with staff and Councillors. He kept the Labour Group very much under his control. I did learn from this that you should let people have a little bit more freedom to speak. I must be honest and say that John and I had many rows. With me being cheeky I sometimes said 'no I don't agree with that' and of course I had to explain myself. But John was a good leader and I've got to pay tribute to him. I always be grateful for what he said to me when he was retiring from Wear Valley Council. He said: 'Well, Brown' - he always called me Brown – 'I think you are the only one here to take over from me and I wish you luck'. I was very touched. One of the greatest pleasures I had was when I did became Leader of the Council in 1995 was conferring on John the honour of being the first Honorary Alderman of Wear Valley. If anyone deserved it, John Richardson did. In many ways John was my mentor and a sort of friend, but sometimes he could exasperate me to death!

"JR"

"The Pagoda"

Since 1974, Wear Valley Council had been housed in various buildings and the chance came to have everybody under one roof. The Co-operative store in the centre of Crook closed, and the site became available. We had to demolish the building because it was in such a bad state. Some people wanted us to keep the lovely stone façade, but it was artificial stone and we had to remove the whole lot, which we did. So we got building it the new Council Offices. It was four stories high, and was bound to stick out into Crook landscape. The old Coop had been three stories, but the new building needed a plant room on top. When the new building was going up, people thought 'oh dear, oh dear, what is this?' What people didn't realise that the new Council Offices would be an asset to the town. Most of the people working there would probably shop into the town, and it would bring people into the town centre. The foundation stone was laid by Council Leader John Richardson on the 21st April 1987, and the building was officially opened by Council Chairman George Taylor the following year. This was a purpose-built building, not glamorous, commonly known in Crook as "The Pagoda". It's all open-plan, which is good because everybody has to work together which I think is good for the staff. It was also an advantage in that all the staff were in one building and not several. These old buildings were costing the council a fortune to maintain. They were all getting old, and so we sold them all off . It's so ironic that since then the Co-op has built a large store on the site of one of our old council offices at Highfield.

JR's heart attack

The Labour Party lost control of the Council in 1991 when we were left with only eight Councillors. I was the only one left at Crook, so we were almost literally wiped out as a Party in the town. There were 28 Liberal Democrats out of 40 members, the other four being Independents. It was a bitter pill for some people to swallow, but we live in a democracy and the Liberal Democrats were elected to power. Chris Foote-Wood, Leader of the Liberal Democrats did work hard to make this happen. We had lost a couple of by-elections [Chris: three actually] before this, so I suppose the writing was on the wall telling us that something was wrong. In the early hours after the 1991 election when the Labour Party lost control, John Richardson had a heart attack so unfortunately was unable to take a full part in the first few months of the Liberal Democrat administration. We had to learn to live with the situation, but I have to say that after the first year things began to crumble a little. I suppose people were a bit disillusioned with politics and then they started to say 'oh dear, this or that is not right.

PC Forty-Nine

The controlling group of LibDems suddenly started to disintegrate with one after another "crossing the floor" to join the Independents. I thought this was lovely, and in my capacity as Labour Group Whip, I said I was I was "PC Forty-Nine", directing of the traffic back and forth across the floor. Every time someone moved over to the Independents, we had to have a new committee set-

"PC Forty-Nine"

up. It was absolute madness, they were driving the officers of the council mad by the way they were conducting themselves. However, it's a democracy, and people have to do what they think is right and proper. Later, two LibDems were disqualified for not attending for six months, and we gained those seats in by-elections. There was another by-election due to the unfortunate death in December 1991 of Labour Cllr Albert Seddon. He was replaced by David Kingston. Another Willington Labour councillor, Keith Reid, resigned and he was replaced by Alan Townsend.

Fun and games

I don't know how the LibDem administration managed to carry on, but they did. From our point of view it was fun and games. Being a politician, we did make the most of it. It was new for us, because we had never had this thing before. People were always of one party or the other party: we didn't have people moving around so much, but that was their prerogative. We had some fun at the Liberal Democrats' expense, but they would probably have had fun at our expense if it had been the Labour Party doing the same, but I must say that it was sad it had to go the way it went. Betty Todd took over from Chris Foote-Wood as Council Leader in 1994, but by then we were running up towards the next council elections in 1995. Executive Director Liz Ashness went back to Norfolk where she came from, and so for the few months that were left Planning Director Paul Worsop took over as Chief Executive. I must say by this time I was feeling a little bit sorry for Cllr Foote Wood. He had tried so hard to keep his party together, but he was having to watch everything disintegrate before his eyes. Chris would probably disagree with me on this, but I thought it doesn't bode too well for them in the 1995 elections. We were more than hopeful of getting back into control, and it was an exciting election for me. I could sense the fact that the voters wanted people they knew, and had been in before, to run the Council. When you are in the Labour Party you get a very good grounding in politics and this stood us in good stead. That's one thing about Labour - our solidarity. So we went into the elections with hopes really high. Cllr John Richardson had decided to retire, so that was the end of an era.

Pictures on opposite page:

1.	Alan Brooksbank	11.	Joan Jobson
2.	Barbara Wilkinson	12.	"JR"
3.	Betty Todd	13.	Julienne Hannibel
4.	Bill Wade	14.	June Lee
5.	Bob Middlewood	15.	Margaret Hurst
6.	Charlie Middlewood	16.	Mary Tarren
7.	"Cherry" Fawcett	17.	Olive Brown
8.	Chris Wood	18.	Teresa Moralee
9.	George Liddell	19.	Tommy Dixon
10.	Jimmy Smith	20.	Tommy Hall

*CFW with Liberal Leader
David Steel MP*

*With LibDem Leader
Paddy Ashdown MP*

*With LibDem Leader Charles
Kennedy MP*

*When were were six
(after three by-election wins)
WVDC LibDem group 1990*

*Three LibDem stalwarts (l-r) Cllrs
Ben Ord, CFW, Gary Huntington*

*Alan Beith MP with Chris &
granddaughter Emily at her home in
Eldon Lane*

Me and my shadow – Olive with Council Vice Chairman Cllr Albert Seddon 1982

Olive and Ken, Queen's Garden Party, Buckingham Palace 1981

Presentation, Crook & Willington Swimming Club, Cllr Denis Harburn on left

Judging Fancy Dress – Olive came as a Council Chairman

Olive lays the foundation stone at the Royal Corner, Crook, 22nd April 1982

Chairman Olive with picture

CFW with (l-r) Cllrs Tommy Dixon, Charlie Hopper, Albert Seddon 1982

King James CA Quiz Team, County Champions (team captain – CFW)

Christmas card youngsters

Guest speaker Cyril Smith MP with his mother, brother, Chris and Frances, Civic Ball 1977

Guest Speaker Denis Healey MP, Civic Ball 1982

Chris with Frances and his late father Stanley Wood, Civic Ball 1977

Cllr Rita Richardson, Olive and Ken 1981

63

*Three Civic Heads: Jacques Laloe
(Mayor of Ivry), Olive Brown
(Chairman of Wear Valley), Dieter Furst
(Burgermeister, Bad Oeynhausen)*

*Meeting Bad Oeynhausen
Burgermeister Dieter Furst, Jimmy
Smith on left*

*Olive gives her speech in fluent
French, amusing Mayor Laloe. Ken:
what is she saying?*

*Cllr Jimmy Smith signs the
Partnerschaft agreement with Bad
Oeynhausen 1977*

Citizen of Honour, Ivry-sur-Seine

*Burgermesiter Willie Spelker makes
his point*

Olive in Europe

Hilary Armstrong MP, Olive, Seamus Murphy

Olive with the German Economics Minister

Mrs Gibson presents a Vase on behalf of the people of Chernobyl

CFW with LibDems Lord Graham Tope, Flo Clucas, Ruth Coleman

LibDem group spokesman CFW at the EU Committee of the Regions

Chris with friend and fellow-spokesman Rosario Condorelli

CFW in Stockholm with ELDR President Annemie Neyts-Uyttebroeck

Chris congratulated by Traian Basescu, Mayor of Bucharest

Exchanging business cards with Traian Basescu, soon to be President of Romania

*Order! Order! George Thomas MP,
Speaker of the House of Commons,
gets the drinks in*

*Hair and teeth much in evidence,
Tony Blair MP signs in*

*Labour Leader Neil Kinnock MP,
Olive with red rose*

*Hilary Armstrong MP, in white suit,
makes a point*

*Dame Thora Hird (centre, in white
hat) causes a stir in Weardale 1982*

Olive with Clare Short MP

67

Ellis Armstrong as Father Christmas 2000

Cllr Belle Bousfield makes a point as Olive & Ken look on

Such a nice boy – Peter Beardsley with (l-r) Cllrs Belle Bousfield, Margaret Pinkney and Olive Brown

Three first ladies of Wear Valley 2003 (l-r) Cllr Margaret Douthwaite, Cllr Olive Brown, Cllr Margaret Jones

Doing the day job – CFW reporting the 2002 Commonwealth Games in Manchester

Chris and good friend Heinz Bocke in Bad Oeynhausen 2007

Plenary session in Brussels, April 2006

CFW raising the Union Flag in Bad Oeynhausen with Burgermeister Klaus Mueller-Zahlmann 2007

Triathlon involves 1500m swim...   *...40k bike...*   *...10k run*

| Stanley Wood | Helen Wood | John Wood |
| Mrs Brigham (Ellen Wood's Mum) | Chris Wood | Ellen Wood |

Wood family 1945

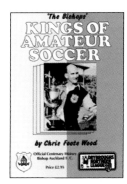

Kings of Amateur Soccer 1986

Chris with son Nick on a holiday trip

Olive MBE with Ken and Diane,
Buckingham Palace 2007

Frances Foote Wood OBE 1992

Olive and Ken on their wedding day
28th July 1962

Chris and Frances, wedding day 2nd
June 1977, picture taken in Cockton
Hill's "Titty-Bottle Park" opposite
the Register Office

Chris and Frances celebrate their
30th wedding anniversary 2007

Good friends, Olive and Diane

Big news – CFW stands down after 40 years

Kids come to the Council

Launching the Wear Fit Club 1991, CFW is No.1 member. We sign up 13,000 members

Wear Valley District Council 1977

Wear Valley District Council 1997

Wear Valley District Council 2004

Proud moment: Olive & Chris receive their Alderman citations from Council Chairman Cllr Eddie Murphy 2007

Olive and Chris dancing together – "JR" was livid!

Chris and Olive, back in the Council Chamber 2009

Chapter Eleven

Chris: Consequences

We lose office; "Immigrant!"; Chance for millions missed; Leisure Centres;
The Pagoda; Threats of violence; Police investigations

We lose Office

My first term as Leader ran from 1976 to 1979 when the local elections
coincided with the general election, and Labour got back into power in Wear
Valley just as Margaret Thatcher took power at Westminster. Labour remained
in control of the Council for a further twelve years. JR, who prior to 1976 had
treated me with utter contempt, now treated me with utter contempt and utter
hostility. He "had a go" at me at virtually every Council meeting. He was vicious
in his language. JR would constantly call me a "fool", a "clown", an "idiot",
"stupid" and so on and so forth. Whatever I said, he would ridicule. We were
both present at a social occasion, when JR made a speech about football. He
described a shot that went high over the bar. 'If Foote Wood had been reporting
the game, it would have been a daisy-cutter', he sneered. That was the way he
was, and I'm sorry that a man who was in power and in complete control of the
Council, should feel it necessary to constantly denigrate a sincere and dedicated
member of the Council, who only wanted to exercise his democratic rights and
represent the people who voted for him.

After one such tirade, JR turned to his Deputy and said: 'I'm sick of
hammering him' – but he could not stop himself. *[Olive: When I was Group
Whip, and we were going into meetings, I often used to say to JR: 'for goodness
sake, calm down, let Foote Wood have his say. At the end of the day, we have the
majority to defeat him on a vote. He always said "all right, Olive, I will", but
as soon as Chris started to speak, JR lost his temper and that was that'.]* Yet JR
could also say the right thing. At the centenary remembrance ceremony in 1996
for the mining disaster that occurred at Brancepeth Colliery on 13th April 1896,
when twenty lives were lost in a pit explosion, JR spoke movingly of the men
and boys who had been killed. 'We shall not see their like again,' he said, exactly
what was needed.

When I was allowed to speak in the Council Chamber, I was rarely able to
complete what I was saying. Very often, JR, or one of his acolytes, or one of the
Council officers, would interrupt me and start an argument. Council meetings
were almost always unpleasant. On numerous occasions a motion would be
passed "that Councillor Foote Wood be no longer heard". In other words, I was

not allowed to speak any further at that meeting. These motions were passed quite often, but always without rhyme or reason. My only "crime" was to disagree with JR, which to him was virtually a capital offence. He just could not take any opposition whatsoever, and he would use whatever verbal ammunition came to hand. I once made the mistake of mentioning to a supposedly friendly Labour councillor that I had been born in Cheshire. This gave JR another stick to beat me with. From then on I was "the Cheshire cat". That may not sound such a terrible thing to say, but the way the words came out of JR's mouth, it was like a curse. He even made fun – in a nasty way - of my house "Wor Hoos".

"Immigrant!"

A word that JR often used for me, and also for Conservative Councillor Margaret Hurst, was "immigrant". This is an absolutely appalling term to use, but JR not only used it, he used it viciously as a term of abuse. JR's attitude was: 'anybody who doesn't live in the village where they were born isn't worth a light'. Not only would he call me an "immigrant", he would make such sneering remarks as 'if you buy the ticket, I'll put you on the train to take you back to where you came from'. The fact that I had chosen to settle in Bishop Auckland and had made my home here, brought up my children here, and become a local Councillor, meant absolutely nothing to him. Margaret Hurst, like me, was brought up in Lancashire and made her home in Bishop Auckland. To JR, she was also an "immigrant" and he said so. What am I to make of a Council Leader who persistently descended to such levels of personal abuse?

Chance to make millions missed

We lost control in 1979 and JR returned for another twelve years of unbridled power. As well as putting a huge financial burden on the backs of the Wear Valley ratepayers and council-tax payers, JR missed the opportunity of income. I well remember a meeting held at the derelict Goods Yard in Bishop Auckland. British Rail wanted to sell off the land, a prime site in the centre of the town, and they gave Wear Valley Council the first option to buy. As I recall, it was for a mere £35,000. JR got on the top of a pile of stone, looked around and said 'we don't want this rubbish'. And that was the end of that. If I had been Leader, we would have snapped up this bargain, and the District Council and the local council taxpayers would have benefitted by – in my estimation – at least a million pounds a year. If I could negotiate a deal for the Newgate Centre which netted us at least £200,000 a year, I'm absolutely certain that I could have negotiated a deal with Morrisons and others which would have brought Wear Valley Council at least £1m year, which for the past twenty years would have meant an extra twenty million pounds income into the Council's coffers. JR refused this opportunity out of sheer parochial prejudice. If it wasn't taking place in Willington, or at least in Crook, then JR wasn't interested. He would never agree to any major developments at Bishop Auckland. But you can't explain this to the voters at election time, people simply do not believe you. People must vote for whom they want, and if they vote for a Labour council that acts in the way it did, then so be it. There's a saying that we get the government that we deserve. Had I been given more time as Leader of Wear Valley, I believe there is so much more that could have been done for the benefit of the District. But I would say that, wouldn't I?

Leisure Centres
Apart from his behaviour in the Council Chamber, I have another major criticism of John Richardson as Council Leader. JR could only think about spending public money, not saving it. Under his rule, three major leisure centres at Bishop Auckland, Crook and Willington, were developed within a few miles of one another, a crazy decision for a small District Council. And the Council's Leisure Department was created from scratch and built up to forty staff, all a huge drain on the Council's resources.

"The Pagoda"
Another expensive decision was to buy the old Co-op at Crook and develop the new Civic Centre there. *[Olive: I agreed with this decision, and so did most of the Labour Group. We were not coerced by JR. We felt the Council needed to be under one roof, and the cost of maintaining old offices in several locations was escalating].* I did agree that it was better in principle for the Council to have one set of offices, rather than several, scattered around, but we could have built a perfectly adequate set of Council offices on land we already owned for around half a million pounds, instead of buying the Co-op, demolishing it, and putting up the ugly and expensive Pagoda at around four million, including a big bill for under-pinning. All JR's extra expenditure was financed by extra borrowing, and in the case of the Pagoda by going to Swiss banks and paying well above the standard rate of interest. This massive additional borrowing resulted in Wear Valley having a debt of nearly fifty million pounds, the highest "per capita" debt of any District Council in the country. To service this debt, we were paying two million pounds a year in interest payments alone, which out of a budget of around ten million represented twenty percent of our income.

Threats of violence
In addition to the personal abuse, there were sometimes threats of physical violence. On one occasion JR threatened: 'I'll throw you through that window'. On another occasion, a Labour councillor came rushing across the Council Chamber, making to hit me and swearing that he would 'put me six foot under'.

"The Pagoda"

Fortunately for him, two of his colleagues grabbed hold of him at the last second and pulled him back. On several other occasions, the Council passed a resolution to remove me from all committees "forthwith" – another way of silencing me - for something I said, even on one occasion when all I did was to quote the words of a Labour councillor. Although I was Leader of the Liberal Group, JR wouldn't allow me to be on the Council's policy committee. He put another Liberal in my place, saying 'he can always resign if he wants', but there was no point as there was no way that JR would allow me on that committee. It was only when the Conservative government brought in the proportional representation on Council committees, that I was able to be a member of this important one. On another occasion JR found out I was going to a conference and cancelled my attendance, even though I had booked to go and had already paid for my wife's accommodation and for her to take part in the conference as an observer. And JR could be extremely petty. When we took control in May 1976, I became Leader and also Chairman of the Council. After every Council AGM, a commemorative photograph is taken of the full Council. JR refused to be in the photograph with me as the newly-installed Chairman, and he ordered the Labour members to boycott the photograph also. To their credit, some – Olive among them - ignored his order.

People might think that I bear a grudge against JR – I don't. I do blame him for the massive financial burden that he put on the Council and people of Wear Valley, and I condemn how he operated in such a dictatorial way, not only with me and other members of the opposition, but also with his own members and Council officers. JR was well known for his outbursts. As chief executive Alan Dobson once said to me as he was about to go in and see JR: 'I've got my tin hat on!' I spent a large part of my early life as a convinced Christian, and I still hold to the principle that you should "hate the sin, love the sinner". I feel sorry for JR. He could have had everything he wanted, all the power and all the glory, but without the nastiness, but he constantly chose to employ the unpleasant side of his nature as a political weapon.

Police investigations

In these twelve years, 1979-1991, WVDC – under JR's direction - made several complaints against me to the Police, once to the Director of Public Prosecutions, twice to my trades union (the National Union of Journalists) and once to the Press Council. Not one of these accusations ever came to anything.

Chapter Twelve

Olive: First Woman Leader

Victory and the Leadership; The "Likely Lads"; An end to "Them and Us";
"Things can only get better"; Chernobyl exchange; Belle's Christmas Card

Victory and the Leadership

The 1995 election was very exciting. When I was at the count I thought at one point that we were going to take all forty seats. In the end we finished with thirty-five Labour Councillors out of forty, two Liberal Democrats and three Independents. I couldn't believe just how many councillors we had managed to get. Everyone in the Labour Party was quite flabbergasted but obviously very pleased. I went to the Labour Group Meeting in great trepidation, but I was elected as Labour Group Leader and Council Leader. I was thrilled – it was a great honour. Cllr Neil Stonehouse from Coundon was elected as my Deputy and Mrs Betty Harker as Secretary of the Labour Group. The unfortunate thing was that Betty Harker died later that year. The by-election saw Labour candidate June Marshall elected to take her place, so we still had our huge majority. There was yet another by-election when, quite incredibly, June Marshall died the following year. But May 1995 was a very good time for me. We had a lot of inexperienced councillors who hadn't been on the council, so I had to help them out. But they soon learned how to go on and how to do things properly. I will never forget walking into the Council Chamber for the annual meeting and seeing all the Labour Party people there and thinking 'my goodness!' It was a very good thing to see, but I knew there would be difficulties because the majority of the Councillors were new. But they really did learn quickly and I was very proud of them. We had a good mix of people and they all gelled in together. The future was looking really, really good. Among these new councillors were eleven women. Wear Valley has always had a good representation of women Councillors. I was pleased, because it gives a different dimension to the Council. We had several experienced women councillors, Belle Bousfield and June Lee among them.

The "Likely Lads"

After the annual Council meeting in May 1995, two members of the Labour Group, Cllr Brian Myers from Willington and Cllr Wilf Dobinson from Crook, came to the Leader's Room to see me. They said: 'Leader, we are appointing ourselves as your "Minders"'. I burst out laughing, and said: 'You would be better named as "The Likely Lads" than Minders!' Everyone seemed to be so happy and carefree, looking forward to being back in control of the Council again. We said we were embarking on a great new venture, and we are all looking forward to having a Labour government again. Because of our outstanding victory in Wear Valley, we felt we were leading the way to a great Labour victory in the General Election, whenever it was called. We won all by-elections where we were seeking to replace Labour candidates in those wards. I remember a By-Election in the Bishop Auckland Town ward which the LibDems won. Chris remarked: 'Thank goodness we've regained this seat!' *[Chris: this by-election was caused by the resignation of the so-called "Caribbean Councillor" who was originally elected as a LibDem, but defected to the Independents before going to live in the West Indies, returning to the UK once every six month so he could still claim his Council Allowances].*

An end to "Them and Us"

I vowed when I took over as Leader in 1995 that I would get rid of this "Them and Us" situation. That is, we would all be Wear Valley and that hopefully it would merge into one as Wear Valley, not Bishop Auckland, Crook, Willington etc. and I think I went a long way to achieving that. The Chairman of the Council was Cllr Tom Judd, deputy chairman was Cllr Sid Dent. I took the chair of Finance with Neil Stonehouse as deputy chairman. Richard Langham was Chairman of Environmental Services, with Cllr Charlie Kay as his deputy. Alan Townsend was Planning Chairman, Cllr Barbara Laurie vice-chairman; Belle Bousefield was chair of Economic Development & Tourism, with Cllr White as vice chair. June Lee chaired the Technical Committee with Wilf Dobinson as deputy. Paul Worsnop left, and we appointed Carole Hughes in his place as chief executive. She had a degree in administration and local government law. It was a good appointment because Carole was local. She had lived in Crook and I knew her very well. We used to play together when we were girls, although she was a bit younger than me. I knew her family well, but that's beside the point. Carole Hughes was appointed on her merits because she was a very good officer. She had Wear Valley stamped right through her heart, I can tell you. Another deputy leader of the Labour Party, Margaret Beckett, was the guest of honour at Tommy Judd's civic ball in February 1996. We've had a number of well-known and distinguished people come to Wear Valley civic balls, Cyril Smith, Paddy Ashdown and Neil Kinnock among them. I had Denis Healey for my Civic Ball, and soon after I became Leader Prince Charles came to Bishop Auckland to open the new railway station and I had the honour of meeting him on another wonderful day.

"Things can only get better"

The council's next Chairman was Cllr Sid Dent, very well known in Bishop Auckland. Sid really enjoyed the role of Councillor and he certainly enjoyed his year as Chairman. The next year, 1997, was a year that we will never forget. We knew there was going to be a general election and of course we were all excited about it. My friend Cllr Belle Bousfield was elected Chairman of the Council that particular year. The general election was announced and as we know the Labour Party had an overwhelming victory, a really overwhelming victory. I will never forget the excitement as I went out after the count. I went to the Town Hall at Bishop Auckland and heard all the results coming in. The excitement was electric, absolutely electric. I will never forget walking out in Crook the next day when everybody came flocking to me saying 'My God, wonderful, wonderful, the future's going to be great'. But I said you know you have got to give people time, but everyone was so excited and it was a really wonderful atmosphere. I've never experienced anything like it.

Chernobyl exchange

In about 1996, Mrs Gibson from Crook saw an advert in the Northern Echo, asking if anyone would take a child from Chernobyl. She answered the advert, and a young person came over to Crook for a visit and was hosted by Mr & Mrs Gibson. Two years later, a group of twenty children came with their leader Svitlana Shuelaea. Mrs Gibson rang me as Leader of the Council to see if they could visit the Council. It was a great pleasure for me to meet these children. We also gave them concessions to use the Council's leisure facilities and they were thrilled to bits. I met with groups of these people and Svitlana until I retired as Leader of WVDC. The link is still ongoing, and there is an excellent charity in Crook called "Children of Chernobyl". I will never forget the excited faces of these children, and I hope we helped then to forget their terrible and traumatic experiences.

Belle's Christmas Card

As Council Chairman, Belle Bousefield decided to run a competition amongst school children to design a Christmas card for herself and myself and for the Chief Executive of the Council. I thought this was a wonderful idea because it got school kids involved in doing things that perhaps they would have not looked forward to doing. But Belle's idea came up trumps. The children took part enthusiastically, and we showed off the cards with the kids and with Santa Claus there. Ellis Armstrong was "Santa" for many years, doing an excellent job. This set a precedent for every other Wear Valley Council Chairman to keep this going. The kids really enjoyed it, and we invited the families to come, grandparents and teachers. I took this Christmas card idea to the Committee of the Regions and it was taken up by the Italians. This was a thing that Cllr Belle Bousefield wanted to do with the advent of the Labour government in 1997. We were hoping that things would change and that as a Council we would get something better from the Labour government. We were looking forward to the future, we had a new administration at Crook as well as at Westminster. There was a buzz about the place.

Our two local MPs, Hilary Armstrong and Derek Foster, both came to see me to have a little chat about things. Everyone was on top form because we all thought 'this is a new era, and let's hope that it will be good for our people and also for the country'. There were comments about Wear Valley Council having a woman Leader, a woman Chief Executive, and a woman Chairman. I responded by saying that we had all reached these positions on our merits and not because we were women. I do not believe in women being pushed forward into positions unless on merit. It was a difficult period for local councils because with the new government taking over in 1997 we had to listen and find out what they wanted us to do. There was a change of values, and it was a bedding-down time for the government as well for local councils.

Chapter Thirteen

Chris: We Win Again

JR has a heart attack; Streamlining the Council; "Our Living Dale";
Wear Fit Club; Bishop Auckland Town Hall; Unmade Streets, Speech Therapy

JR has a heart attack

I would never descend to JR's level – I believe in "do as you would be done by",
not "an eye for an eye". To prove my point: in 1991 we won a massive victory,
with us LibDems winning twenty-eight out of forty seats on the Council,
sweeping Labour out of power. In the early hours following that election, JR
suffered a heart attack and was in intensive care. I immediately said that I would
not conduct any press interviews while JR was in the hospital. I am very
competitive and I like to win, but I do not believe in crowing over someone you
have defeated at any time, much less when your opponent is gravely ill. So I did
not make the most of our triumph, I refused many interviews and appearances
on radio and television, out of respect if you will. In the years that followed
when I was Leader of the Council, never once did I give JR any verbal abuse,
nor did any of my colleagues. All members of the opposition – and all Liberal
members of course – were allowed to speak freely and were never interrupted
except on a genuine point of order, and that rarely.

Unlike JR, I have always treated all members with respect, however they
treated me. For the first time in twelve years, there was genuine democracy in
the Council Chamber. And there was also an end to parochialism on the Council.
As Leader I made sure that every part of the District was dealt with fairly,
regardless of who represented each ward. Under JR, Labour-held wards were
always considered before the rest, Willington first, then Crook, then Tow Law
and Weardale, and Bishop Auckland last of all. Under my leadership, the
Council allocated "Wear Valley Action" money to every ward strictly on a
population basis, which the local members could then decide to spend as they
wished, for proper purposes of course. That applied equally to all members,
regardless of Party. While giving Bishop Auckland its proper due, I brought
Willington to the fore as a prime development point, and revived plans for the
Crook By-Pass, all but forgotten under Labour.

Streamlining the Council

When we came into office in 1991, we had a massive task. We set about
restoring the Council's finances, greatly reducing its huge deficit and thus
reducing interest payments, maintaining services while at the same time keeping

84

down rates and rent rises to affordable levels. I believe we were successful in all these important matters. We massively streamlined the internal organisation of the Council. We halved the number of committees from ten to five, and vastly reduced the number of sub-committees, from fifty-two to five. In my view, the only reason that all these committees and sub-committees had been set up was to hand out more jobs to Labour members as chairs and vice-chairs, and to allow members to come to meetings every day of the week if they wished and thereby claim their relatively meagre attendance allowance - ten pounds a day if I recall correctly. We also reintroduced evening meetings to allow working Councillors and members of the public to attend. We introduced the principle of public speaking at Council meetings, something that has been a great success. When members of the public are allowed to speak at Council meetings, they feel they are putting their case directly to the Councillors who make the decisions. They have their day in court, as it were, so even if the result eventually goes against them, they are more inclined to accept it. We decided to take the Council "on the road," and have full Council meetings in all parts of the district. This also proved extremely popular, and we held Council meetings at Wolsingham, Stanhope and Bishop Auckland, for example, which attracted scores of the public.

"Our Living Dale"
As Council Leader, I gave Weardale its proper due. Even before our 1991 success, I had produced a policy paper entitled "Our Living Dale", the first time any political party had done anything of this nature. In contrast to the relative neglect of the Dale under JR, I introduced many schemes of improvement. As Council Leader, I made it my business to visit Weardale regularly, having an average of two formal or informal meetings a week in Weardale in 1991-92 alone. One example: with the help and advice of my friend and colleague Cllr Maurice Almond, I brokered a scheme to remove the burden of maintaining the St John's Chapel Market Place from the voluntary Town Hall committee with a complete refurbishment scheme. It was then taken over for future maintenance by the highway authority, the County Council. We helped refurbish all three town halls in the Dale, at Wolsingham, Stanhope and St John's Chapel. We put more money into the swimming pools at Wolsingham and Stanhope, saving the latter (open-air pool) from closure. We changed the day of the week when the District Council's Planning Committee met to avoid clashing with Parish Council meetings, allowing Parish Councillors to attend. We designated a liaison officer to deal with Parish and Town Councils, and we gave the biggest-ever Council subsidy to the two Dales Parish Councils. We bought Stanhope Station, a much-criticised decision without which the revival of the Bishop Auckland to Stanhope Railway would have been almost impossible. When the Bishop Auckland to Eastgate rail line was closed, the urgent action which I

Chris still keeps fit

instituted as Leader to prevent the line being taken up and the land sold off –
both of which were imminent - made the restoration of the line possible. Against
the advice of officers, we fought and won the "Battle of Jenny's Cottage",
winning the right for redundant farm buildings to be converted into residential
accommodation, thus removing dereliction and providing affordable homes in
the Dale.

Wear Fit Club

When I came in again as Leader in 1991 – and I am very much a "hands-on"
Leader - I did my best to maximise the use of the Council's expensive leisure
facilities by creating and promoting the "Wear Fit" Club, which we built up to a
massive 13,000 members. Attendances at Wear Valley's Leisure Centres have
never been greater before or since. Another thing I was able to do was to
facilitate Bishop Auckland Rugby Club in buying the 13-acre former
Waterworks site by the River Wear, and I was immensely proud to be asked to
officially open their new clubhouse. We also helped the Rugby Club get its
electricity supply when this was proving a stumbling-block. We helped the
Durham Cheshire Home relocate from Consett to purpose-built premises in
Crook. As well as approving the development, we gave the Home a new address,
Worthington Close, after the late husband of the main organiser Mrs
Worthington, and at her request. Our first LibDem Council Chairman, Maurice
Almond, devoted his Chairman's Charity to the Home, and we were both at the
official opening by film star and raconteur Peter Ustinov. By a huge irony, my
son Nick is now a resident of the Crook Cheshire Home, where the staff care for
him very well. Nick, then 38, was in full health and working in London in 2001
when he suffered a sudden stroke, a massive brain haemorrhage leaving him
paralysed down one side and unable to speak. He was flown to the specialist
brain unit at Southampton, undoubtedly saving his life. After treatment there –
he was in a coma for several days – and at Middlesbrough, Nick lived in a care
home at Consett before moving to Crook. Nick goes out and about in his electric
wheelchair, and – to my great delight - he was recently elected to the Cheshire
Home residents' committee in a three-way contest. My granddaughter Emily
was elected to her School Council in Wolsingham when she lived there, so it
must be in the blood!

Bishop Auckland Town Hall

Some people have disputed our role as a Party in saving Bishop Auckland Town
Hall. All I can do is to tell you what we did, and let you judge for yourselves.
We started it, and we finished it. In 1989, the Town Hall was in a dreadful state,
derelict and cordoned off as a dangerous building. There was a very real danger
that this historic building in the centre of the Market Place would have to be

demolished. Prior to that, all the furniture and fittings had been taken out, and the Council Chamber destroyed – I can't put it any other way – to become part of what is now the Laurel Room. The building was put up for sale, and the Council agreed to sell it to Gary Gibson, the then chairman of Hartlepool United Football Club. Gibson claimed that he could restore the Town Hall and make it profitable. Not only did we LibDems strongly dispute this claim, we were also totally opposed to the Town Hall falling into private hands. Once sold, the building might have been restored by Gibson as he claimed, or it could have been demolished and the site redeveloped. Once the Town Hall was in private hands, the Council would have little control over its future. And what if it fell down anyway? Two things were needed to save the Town Hall, restore it and keep it in public ownership: one was to stop the sale to Gibson (or anyone else) and the other was to start a campaign to save Bishop Auckland's most iconic building. We LibDems did both – and it was our decisions as a majority Council Group that ensured its eventual restoration was carried out.

It was at a meeting of the Bishop Auckland LibDems in the Wear Valley Hotel that we decided to start a campaign to save the Town Hall and to raise a public petition. I designed and printed the petition forms, choosing the wording very carefully: "to restore Bishop Auckland Town Hall and maintain it in public ownership". This latter part of the petition was essential, as without it the (Labour-controlled) Council could sell off the Town Hall and claim they had "saved" it. Some people who wanted to save the Town Hall actually welcomed the Council's decision to sell it to Gary Gibson. In our view, that would have been a fatal error, and the Town Hall would have been lost. Frances organised the petition from start to finish, let no-one have any doubt about that. She put in an enormous amount of work and succeeded in gaining 10,000 signatures. Of course many people, LibDem members and others, came forward to help with the petition, but we organised it.

We also organised the first public protest meeting in King James I School. I chaired the meeting, along with LibDem Cllr Marie Land. We invited Labour, Conservative and Independent councillors to join us on the stage, as we wanted it to be an all-Party campaign, but they all refused. Later public meetings were chaired – at our request - by an independent chairman, Dr. Bob McManners, who later presented the petition to the Council. We wanted the campaign to be open to people of all Parties and of none, as indeed it was from the start. But we started both the campaign and the petition.

Not only that, if we had not won a LibDem majority on the Council in 1991, I am convinced that Bishop Auckland Town Hall would not have been saved, let alone fully restored. It is true that the Labour Council had a last-minute change of heart, allowing JR to get his name on a Town Hall plaque which remains to this day. When we won control of the Council, Carole Hughes – later to become the Council's chief executive - asked me if I was going to have JR's plaque taken down. I said 'no, I am not that petty-minded'. The fact was that the money Labour "set aside" for the restoration of the Town Hall (half a million pounds) would have been wholly inadequate for what turned out to be a £4m scheme with only minor grant aid. If Labour had retained power on Wear Valley Council in 1991, I am absolutely convinced that JR, with his anti-Bishop Auckland attitude, would have abandoned the scheme as being too expensive. But winning a LibDem majority on the Council was just the start – then we had to vote the money to do the job, and that took determination and courage by every LibDem councillor who supported the scheme (some didn't, and said so). But we found the money, we voted it through, and we completed the scheme. Public meetings, letters to the newspapers and petitions – even of 10,000 signatures – all help a campaign like this to succeed, but without the support and commitment of a political majority on the Council to make the necessary decisions, and the determined leadership to make it all happen, nothing would have been done.

Unmade Streets
Over the years, I have been involved in getting unmade streets made up in many parts of the District. The hardest job of all was to get unmade streets made up in the Dene Valley, but we achieved it. Eventually, after years and years of hard toil and struggle by me and my ward colleague Geoff Harrison, we got the streets in Eldon Lane made up. Did the people thank us for it? Not a bit. Despite the fact that it was abundantly clear that we could only get the streets done in one village at a time, and that only with great difficulty, we got nothing but complaints from all the other villages in the Dene Valley as to why they hadn't been done first. At the next election, Geoff lost his seat – by two votes – and I only just held on to mine. Yet for all the improvements in the Dene Valley, none of it would have been possible had Geoff and I not won national and EU funding for the area's redevelopment schemes. Officers and members alike told me it was "impossible" to get European ex-coalfield funding for the Dene Valley, where the pits had closed forty years or more before (JR had tried and failed), but get it we did. We were told the Dene Valley would not qualify for Rural funding (JR didn't even try), but get it we did, and for other parts of the District too.

Speech Therapy
For 35 of the 40 years of my time as a district councillor, I was a school governor and Chairman of Governors for most of that time. School governors do not get a penny in expenses or allowances - the same applies to Parish Councillors, of

which I was also one for several years - something the critics of local councillors never acknowledge. They wouldn't do it for nothing, yet they accuse those of us who do do it for nothing of "making money" out of it. Funny old world, isn't it? I was a governor of Eldon lane School for around twenty years, and fought many battles on the school's behalf. One of the biggest battles was to get the help needed for our under-achieving children. Despite the fact that we had a bigger proportion of ESN children in our school than any other, Eldon Lane was the only primary school in the district without a special assistant to help our one (over-worked) teacher who gave extra tuition to these youngsters a few hours a week. It took two delegations to County Hall to see the Director of Education to get some action. Typically, after our first meeting – when we were promised the extra help we needed – nothing whatsoever happened for months. Officials at County Hall were "protecting their budgets". So we had to go again and make the same case for a second time before anything happened.

One battle we lost was over speech therapy. For a time I used to take children for reading, and I was well aware that a high proportion of children at our school needed help with their speech. If a child cannot make themselves understood, they have difficulty learning. Yet the Health Trust unilaterally withdrew the speech therapy service they had provided for years – and without bothering to tell us! Once more I led a delegation to plead our cause, but to no avail. It was "budgets" again. Turning to the Education Authority (the County Council) to replace our lost service, again we were stymied. Even if money could be found to fund the service, we were told, there is a shortage of speech therapists. With Health Authorities paying a higher rate than local councils, the County could not fill those posts – and they could not raise the salaries they offered. "Budgets" yet again.

Chapter Fourteen

Olive: Always room for improvement

Best Value; An Excellent Council

Best Value

It seemed no time atall when we were facing another local election, in 1999. Although we had won three by-elections in the meantime, we were still wondering what was going to happen. However, we were very lucky and we did again win a substantial majority. This was my first election as Leader and I was really pleased and proud that we did manage to win another term of office for us on the Council. It promised to be a difficult time, because the government was already talking about Best Value which I agreed with. Making Councils take a look at themselves and see what they were doing was a very good idea, although every Council thought they were very good, indeed brilliant. These Best Value inspections came in 2001.

Before that we had the Millennium year of 2000 when we went into the twenty-first century. Everybody was on tenterhooks because there was a danger that the new technology computers might break down when 2000 came in. So every council had to have backups done in case everything crashed. Anyhow, it all went smoothly. We welcomed in the year 2000 with a champagne cork popping, not a bang or a crash. But it was also a sad year. Carole Hughes had been ill for a while and sadly died. Again the Council was left with no chief executive. Finance Officer Eddie Scrivens took over for a while, but we had to look for a new Chief Executive and we appointed Iain Phillips from York. I missed Carole very much because she had Wear Valley written through her heart.

The government was talking about having inspections to see if we were up to scratch. Wear Valley's Housing Department got a really bad Best Value report, as did the refuse collection service. We were all very upset about it, especially about housing. We nearly had direct intervention by government, but just managed to avoid that by taking action ourselves. So in 2001 Cllr Belle Bousefield was elected Chairman of Housing. This was a first-class decision, because Belle had housing right at her heart. We also had a new Housing Officer. We needed to have a new outlook on everything, and we appointed Michael Lang from Gateshead. These adverse reports made us realise we weren't as good as we thought we were. We had to do the four C's: compare, compete, challenge and communicate. My favourite was communicate because I have always said we must communicate with the public, with the staff and with everybody on the Council. If you can't communicate with people, you can't compare, you can't compete and you can't challenge.

An Excellent Council

In May 2001 Sedgefield MP Tony Blair, now Prime Minister, paid us another visit to open Innovation House. I met him and had a very enjoyable day. After Belle Bousefield's children's Christmas Card competition, we invited the local schools to come, meet the Council and take part in a debate in the Council Chamber. The children liked this very much. During the year 2001 we really did work hard, as did the staff in the housing department and the refuse collection service. We had to improve dramatically. It took us a while to do it, but in the end and we came through and got the two stars that we needed. That wasn't achieved without a lot of heartache and a lot of hard work by the housing department, by the staff and by Cllr Bousefield and her deputy chairmen, first Cllr Margaret Pinkney and then Cllr Margaret Douthwaite. Belle lived for the Council, and she Michael Laing got on very well. All of these inspections were very draining on the Council's resources, but they had to be done. Under Michael Laing's guidance, first as Chief Housing Officer and later as Chief Executive, the Council made excellent progress. After looking at all the options for our council houses, we decided to go for Arms Length Management of our housing stock. This meant a better deal for our tenants. From being a council "likely to improve" we went to an "excellent" council. I must pay tribute to all the chief officers, staff and workforce of WVDC who worked very hard to achieve two stars for our housing service. Perhaps if Councils had been allowed to build more social housing, there would not have been the problems for first-time buyers there are now.

Chapter Fifteen

Chris: Seeds of Destruction

A big majority; Rebellion; Loyal LibDem members; I step down;
Maurice Almond

A big majority

One of our problems from 1991 onwards was our big majority. Whenever you
have a large majority, it becomes all too easy for individuals to go their own way.
While this may sound perfectly democratic, in fact many of the "rebellions"
were for the wrong reasons or no particular reason at all. But as we didn't operate
a Party Whip, this situation was tolerated despite the fact that some members
would come to Group Meetings and agree to a certain course of action, only to
vote against it when it came to the Council meeting. This I found inexplicable.

Another problem was the fact that very few of our councillors had been in
opposition before – they came straight into a situation of control. There's
nothing wrong with that, every one of us has to start some time. And it's not that
a new councillor cannot become a committee chairman or even Chairman of
Council, without previous council experience, as did happen with us. It is simply
that being in opposition teaches you about the facts of life, teaches you about the
realities of how a council works, and I think this was one factor that militated
against us. While I am totally committed to freedom of speech and action, and
have written-in to our constitution that all LibDem councillors have the right to
speak and vote as their consciences dictates, anyone who aspires to office should
accept what is known as "cabinet responsibility". If you become a member of a
controlling group and wish to play a major part in running the Council, ie as a
committee chairman or vice-chairman, you've got to accept collective
responsibility. This does not mean that members should be forced to vote against
their conscience, far from it, but without compromise and general agreement no
organisation can function. I challenge anybody to quote a single instance when
there was a policy disagreement amongst us LibDems during our three years in
power 1991 to 1994. To the best of my knowledge and recollection, every single
time a councillor defected from our ranks, it was not for policy reasons.

Rebellion

And so our term in office last only three years instead of four. JR, who had had
very little to say during those three years, and had not put forward one single
alternative policy to what we were doing, proved what an astute political brain
he has. A secret meeting was held in the Council Chamber between the Labour

and Independent groups and the so-called "rebels". There was only one item on the agenda, and that was to remove Cllr Chris Foote Wood as Leader of the Council. JR was superb. He knew just how much the rebels prized their committee chairmanships. Being a committee chairman gives you prestige, a little bit of power, and a small amount of extra cash. To some members, these positions were their be-all and end-all. So JR stood up and said: 'when they (the rebels) come over, they bring their chairs with them'. In other words, he was promising that if they would combine with him and the Independents to remove me from power, they would be rewarded by being allowed to keep their committee chairmanships. But JR knew exactly what would happen, and he knew that even if he wanted to keep these people as chairmen – which he certainly did not - it was highly unlikely that he would have the power to do so. And so it proved.

Loyal LibDem members

We started 1991 with 28 Councillors. By mid-1994 our group was down to nineteen – less than a majority. Two had been disqualified for not attending council meetings for six months. Three had set up their own breakaway group, and others had defected to the Labour or Independent groups. I will always be grateful to those who stuck loyally by the Party, including Len Carr, Michael Wigley, Geoff Harrison, Alan Anderson, Betty Todd, Alan Hutchinson, Joan Jobson, David English, Richard Groves, Maurice Almond and David Halliday. Cliff Sanderson, John Ferguson and John Chatfield briefly quit the LibDem Group but soon returned.

"A hanging party"

I step down

There was no need to move a vote of no confidence in me as Leader at the next Council Meeting. I believe in our democratic system and I always act accordingly. In the House of Commons, the Prime Minister is the person who has a majority to back him/her. When the PM can no longer command a majority in the House, he or she must go. So I jumped before I was pushed. I must say at this point that the great majority of the LibDem group remained loyal to the Party and to me as their democratically-elected Leader, but by-election losses and defections had reduced us to a minority on the Council. So I immediately stood down as Leader. I could have carried on as head of a minority administration, as had happened since with both Labour and the LibDems, but I thought it was in the best interests of the Party, the Council, and most of all the people of the District, to end the uncertainty and stand down. Although my LibDem colleague Betty Todd was elected as Leader in my place, the Council

"Stabbed in the back"

would not allow her to have a deputy. The Council also refused her the position of Chairman of Policy and Finance, a crucial one for the Leader to hold. In other words, Betty was Leader but had no real power. There followed eleven months of chaos in which no-one was in charge of the Council, and nothing whatsoever was achieved. Various people were elected to chairmanships, but the Labour Party sat on its hands and refused either to nominate any chairmen or vote for them. JR knew exactly what he was doing – causing as much chaos as possible and blaming the LibDems. He didn't start the blaze, but he threw petrol on the flames. Did any one of these people who conspired to get rid of me ever think for a moment of the good of the District?

The irony is this: the rebels thought that by destroying the (democratically-elected) LibDem majority, that they would hold the balance of power on the Council and thus they would rule the roost. If only they had bothered to discuss it with me, I could have told them that this simply would not and could not happen. A small minority cannot bend the will of the majority - and I was proved right. Further to that, at the subsequent election in 1995, every single one of the "rebels" lost his or her seat. The majority of loyal LibDem members also lost their seats, as this was the time of "the Blair Factor", Labour was riding high, and the public simply do not vote for divided parties. And so, after twelve years in opposition and just three more years in power, we were condemned to another twelve years in opposition. That's politics and that's life.

I can and will defend every single decision I made as a Councillor, as Group Leader and as Leader of the Council. I may of course be criticised for those decisions, but I can give cogent reasons why I did what I did. I challenge any one of the "rebels" who deliberately sank our Party in Wear Valley to give a single logical reason for the decisions they made and the actions they took. It is blindingly obvious that these "rebels" simply didn't like my Leadership. They were quite willing to destroy the Party under whose banner they had been elected, simply to get rid of the one person who was very largely responsible for getting them elected in the first place!

"Rebels" dug their own graves

Not liking someone is no reason for quitting a political Party. The fact of the matter is that I was Liberal/LibDem Group Leader on Bishop Auckland UDC and Wear Valley DC for a total of thirty-three years. Every single year we held an election for Group Leader, and in all those thirty-three years I was challenged for the leadership just once. That was in 1994 when Cllr Bill Wade put his name forward, which he was perfectly entitled to do. In the subsequent vote, at a very emotional meeting, I was re-elected as Leader by a two-to-one majority. Everybody was relieved that the decision had been made. Bill Wade and I embraced, he raised my hand and declared I had his 'one hundred percent support' and that we should all unite behind me. Everybody clapped and cheered. We were united once more. Three weeks later, Bill Wade joined the Labour Party. If you lose a democratic vote, as I have many times, you accept the result and get on with it. If you don't get what you want, you don't join another political party and try your luck there.

Where are they now?

Maurice Almond

In a later chapter, Olive has written very movingly about the death of her friend Belle Bousfield and how it affected her. I have had a similar experience with Maurice Almond from Cowshill. Maurice was a hugely effective councillor for the St John's Chapel Ward, and very popular despite being an "incomer". I am sure that, had it not been for him being seriously ill at the time of the 1999 election, he would have retained his seat. Maurice turned up at a public meeting we held in Stanhope, joined the Party and was duly elected in 1991. Maurice was immediately voted in as Chairman of the Council and did an excellent job, only to be undermined by certain individuals – officers and members - who were looking to destabilise our administration. They played on Maurice's lack of experience in council matters, so much so that he was bamboozled into resigning as Council Chairman after only a few months in office. I was told that Maurice was also going to resign as a councillor, thus forcing an unwelcome by-election only a short time after we had taken control. I immediately rang Maurice. "I'm definitely going to resign," he said, "I've made up my mind. An officer's on his way to get my resignation". "Maurice, I'm coming to see you – right now. Don't sign anything until I get there". I jumped into my car and tore up to Cowshill which is at the top end of the Dale. Fortunately, I got there before the officer did. Maurice was adamant he would resign as Chairman – why he allowed himself to be so affected, I will never know – but, much to my relief, he agreed to stay on as a councillor.

After that, Maurice and I became close friends. Although he had been a critic of the extravagances of some councillors on Town Twinning trips, he readily agreed to go with me to visit our twin towns of Ivry-sur-Seine and Bad Oeynhausen, provided we paid all our own expenses – which we both did, another financial sacrifice the critics will never acknowledge. More than once Maurice pulled me out of a hole when – without Frances there to translate – I got myself into bother through my limited knowledge of German. Maurice had been stationed in Germany and spoke the language fluently. Maurice also provided a ready ear for the troubles that always beset a Leader. He would listen, sympathise and, without censure, advise me as to the error of my ways and suggest another route to the desired objective.

It was a great sadness to me when Maurice died, but I was immensely proud to be asked to help arrange his funeral and give the oration. Of course as a journalist I am well capable of writing anything suitable for any occasion, and I tried to give full measure to the life of a man whose mainspring was to help others. But most of all I spoke from the heart. I had lost a friend, a dear, unselfish friend. There was one more service that we – I include my wife Frances in this – were able to render our friend Maurice. He was cremated and we kept his ashes in an urn on our mantelpiece for a week. Then, by arrangement, we took Maurice to his home town in Lancashire where his ashes were interred in the family plot. Only a few of his relatives had been able to attend the first funeral at Durham, and this time there was a full turnout and a proper tea afterwards. It was a hugely moving occasion, and one I will never forget.

Chapter Sixteen

Olive: Taking my seat in Brussels

European representative; Youth Parliament;
Hosting the Education Commission; Bishop's Palace

European representative

2002 was another very important year in my life. On the 25th January I was appointed as a delegate from the North East to the EU Committee of the Regions (CoR) in Brussels. This was something I really wanted to do because I have always had a European perspective and I felt that Wear Valley would be put on the map with me being there. There were three councillors representing the North East on the Committee of the Regions, me, Cllr Michael Davey, Leader of Northumberland County Council, and Cllr George Gill, Leader of Gateshead Council. In Brussels I was appointed to the Education & Culture Commission. This I found most interesting. I was passionately interested in youth and also culture and tourism which I'd already been involved with. In Brussels I spoke quite a lot and made a lot of friends from all over Europe. They all got to know about Wear Valley! In my European work I got a lot of help and good advice from Adrian Stradling, an officer with the North East Assembly, who sometimes came to meetings in Europe [Chris: Adrian was also a big help to me].

Youth Parliament

One of my most enjoyable duties was as part of the CoR Education Commission. I was very much involved with the European Youth Parliament. They had set up a European youth parliament, and the first meeting of this was in Durham City which I was privileged to attend. After that I was involved with the English branch of the European youth parliament. I attended their meetings and tried to encourage our region's youth to take part. I also attended meetings in Brussels and other European capitals. With the English Youth Parliament, I found the young people had no hang-ups about Europe. They wanted to take part in European affairs. In meetings, both here and in Europe, I found their questions and views were uplifting and refreshing.

Hosting the Education Commission

In 2005 I was very privileged to host the CoR's Education Commission here in the North East. Although most of the meetings of the Committee of the Regions are held in Brussels, all the CoR's six Commissions also hold meetings in other EU countries. At my suggestion, the Education Commission, of which I was a member, came to Durham for a full session over two days. There were

99

Councillors, regional representatives and officials from all over Europe and they all thought the Bishop's Palace was absolutely wonderful. They said I lived in a beautiful area and of course Durham City was the jewel in the crown with its historic Cathedral and Castle. We had the formal meeting in the new Gala Theatre in Durham City, and I felt highly privileged to see delegates from all over Europe come to our region.

The main subject of the conference was New Technology, and Cllr Alex Watson, Leader of Derwentside District Council, gave a presentation on how his Council had brought Broadband to Derwentside, the first district to be fully "wired up". I took some of the delegates into the Tourism offices in Durham City to meet the staff. They spent money in Durham and in Bishop Auckland as well, and some said they would come back for a holiday. I always follow things up, so I did pop into the tourist board and they told me they had had a good few enquiries from some people who were coming back over from different places in Europe for holidays. With the help of the North East Assembly and Durham City Council, delegates stayed at hotels in and around Durham City and the main meeting was held in the new Gala Theatre in Durham. All the delegates and officials found these facilities to be first class, and quite a few stayed an extra night to visit Durham Cathedral and Castle, and to explore the Durham countryside.

Bishop's Palace

I was determined that all these important people from around the EU should visit Wear Valley, so I jumped at the chance to host the formal dinner. "We've got the very place," I said, "the Bishop's Palace, Auckland Castle". And so we had this splendid evening in the main hall at Auckland Castle. Everybody was hugely impressed, and for months afterwards, whenever I was in Europe, people were always reminding me what a tremendous experience it was to come to Durham and the Wear Valley. Seamus Murphy from Ireland, President of the CoR Education Commission, was lavish in his praise for the whole visit. At the next meeting in Brussels they all said what a wonderful time they had had, how they thought it was a beautiful area and that they would return. This was putting Wear Valley and the North East on the map. As a region we needed all the publicity we could get because we had had a disappointment. We were all backing Newcastle-Gateshead to be European City of Culture 2008, but unfortunately we lost out to Liverpool. Bruges in Belgium was the City of Culture before Liverpool. I had visited Bruges and saw what had happened there.

Roll on 2005 and an amazing thing happened. Cllr Chris Foote-Wood was also appointed as a member of the Committee of the Regions, the first LibDem from the North East. I kept my place, so two out of the three councillors representing the Nortth East on this important European body came from little Wear Valley! I thought this was a wonderful thing, because I don't think it had ever happened before for two people from one small district to represent a region. We were both very pleased.

Chapter Seventeen

Chris: Back in Opposition

Olive as Leader; I "lose" my seat; Standing Down

Olive as Leader

I must say that when Olive Brown became Leader of the District Council in 1995, there was a completely different atmosphere on the Council. The days of shouting, insulting and threatening the opposition when JR was Leader had long gone. Everyone was allowed to have their say – as was the case under my leadership - and Olive always kept me informed as Leader of the Opposition. Her successor, Cllr Neil Stonehouse, also treated the opposition perfectly fairly, and I have no complaints about the way either of them conducted themselves as Leader of the Council. I did disagree with some of the policies they introduced, and I believe they failed to take action when they could and should have done, but that is another matter altogether and simply democracy. I have always said that the will of the people must be respected. When the public vote to give a particular Party a majority on the Council, then that Party not only has the right but also the duty to run the Council and to determine the policies of the Council for the next four years. The opposition is there to scrutinise, to comment and criticize, to offer their own solutions and to stand by as an alternative government, should the public so wish it, at the next election.

I "lose" my seat

In my 40 years as a District Councillor I've never had a big majority – I tell too many people the truth to be popular - but it was never closer than in 1999 when I actually "lost" my seat at the Town Hall count only to be reinstated an hour later. In the two-seat Dene Valley ward, the two Labour candidates were declared elected and I was out – after 32 years as a Councillor. So I made a conciliatory farewell speech, I congratulated my victorious opponents and wished them well, and I thanked my colleagues and the people of the District for all their support over the years. Then I left the main hall and went into the Laurel room next door to check on all the other results. Meantime, Labour people were running round all the pubs and clubs in the Market Place, bragging and boasting at my defeat. Half an hour later, a Council official came to see me. 'Cllr Foote Wood, you'd better come back in, we've found some spare votes,' he said. 'Are they mine?' I asked, well knowing what the answer would be. This officer acted with honesty, integrity and bravery, and I thank him for it. So there was a recount, or rather two recounts, and I was declared re-elected after all. On a strict point of electoral law, this was quite illegal. Once a Councillor (or MP) has been declared elected, that is it, even if it's obvious there's been a mistake. On three other occasions, I have actually seen it happen. But on this occasion common-sense prevailed, and the previous declaration was overturned. But I do feel sorry for the "victorious" Labour candidate who "won" a seat only to lose it an hour later. Sadly, this was not an isolated occasion of Liberal votes being "mislaid" here in the North East. In my experience, that has happened on at least two other occasions. I have attended at least 100 election counts in my time, so these occurances are thankfully rare – but three is still three too many.

Standing Down

In 2006 I told the LibDem Group that I would not be contesting the District Council elections the following year when I had completed 40 years as a Councillor. I also stood down as Group Leader, for two reasons. One was to ensure a smooth "hand-over" of power to a new Group Leader, and to give that new Leader time to "bed in" and lead the Party into the 2007 elections. In a three-way contest, Cllr John Ferguson, my deputy for the previous six-and-a-half years, was elected as LibDem Group Leader with an overall majority on the first ballot. But, like me, John had his enemies in the Party and the plotters were soon at work again. Although under John's leadership we had an excellent result in the 2007 elections, winning 16 seats (from 11) to 18 for Labour and so removing Labour's majority on the Council, that was not good enough for some. As with me, they were determined to get rid of John Ferguson as Leader, by fair means or foul. And, as with me, they chose foul. Again there were the secret meetings, and John, like me, jumped before he was pushed. Cllr Tommy Taylor was elected as Leader, only to be replaced in 2008 by Cllr Neil Harrison. The plotters had tasted blood, and they wanted more. After Derek Jago and I had both been selected as LibDem candidates for the 2008 elections to the new unitary County Council, they decided to "get rid of us" both, and replace us with their own preferred candidates. My 40 years as a District Councillor and twelve years as a County Councillor, and the fact that I had fought the Town Ward at the previous County Council elections, counted for nothing.

At a Group Meeting, TEN Wear Valley LibDem councillors signed a "round robin" letter saying they would all RESIGN FROM THE PARTY en bloc (and stand as Independents in the forthcoming County Council elections) unless I withdrew as a candidate. Due to a technicality there was a re-run, and so Derek and I were voted out and replaced. At the time of writing, this deplorable episode was still under investigation by the Party.

Chapter Eighteen

Olive: Still work to do

Battle for the ALMO; I lose a dear friend; Coup d'Etat

Battle for the ALMO

After improving our Housing Service to be rated two stars, we had to consider two or three options for the future of our Council Houses. The Council on its own could not raise the finance needed to bring all our houses up to modern standards, so the only practical alternatives were either to sell them to a housing association and have nothing further to do with them or we go for an ALMO - Arms Length Management Organisation. With this, the Council would still have some control in partnership with this new kind of housing association. We balloted the tenants on this, and they voted for the ALMO option. Most wanted to stay with the District Council, but that was not an option. The government had in effect decreed that the Council could not remain in full control of its housing stock. We also set up Tenants Associations wherever we had a lot of council houses. We were very fortunate in getting good people to do this. These dedicated men and women came along and gave their time to improving the stock of our council houses.

We also had yet another inspection, the Comprehensive Performance Assessment (CPA). This was to assess the performance of the whole Council. I had to go in front of the inspectors again and I just felt as though we were being inspected to death. We got a favourable report, 'likely to improve to excellent', so that wasn't too bad. However, we had to get to Excellent and I'm very pleased to say just after I retired from the Council we did notice that we had been rated an Excellent Council. I felt very proud that perhaps some of my efforts did help us to get this 'Excellent' award.

I lose a dear friend

When Belle Bousfield was re-elected to the Council in 1995 (she had lost her seat in 1991) it was like a whirlwind coming in. Belle, a very forthright person, was "on the ball" from day one. She loved her council work and really helped the people in her Wheatbottom/Helmington Row ward. Belle was Chairman of the Council 1997-98 and enjoyed her year of office tremendously. Belle had never flown in her life, but she conquered her fear of flying and visited our two twin towns, Ivry-sur-Seine and Bad Oeynhausen. She enjoyed the experience so much that afterwards she regularly flew to Spain for holidays. Belle became Chairman of the Economic Development Committee in 1999, and two years later Chairman of Housing and it was there that she found her true vocation. The Council's Housing Department had received a bad Inspection Report. We had to improve dramatically, and our aim was achieve a two-star rating as an Excellent Council. Belle, as Housing Chairman, Michael Laing (Chief Housing Officer) and all the Housing Department staff and workforce worked extremely hard. Of the options available, we decided to create an ALMO (Arms Length Management Organisation). Our tenants voted for the ALMO option which is now in being as Dale & Valley Homes. There are Council members on it, members of the Tenants' Association, and members of the public. It hasn't been such a great upheaval to move from Council ownership to "arms length management". It's now up and running and going well. I must again pay tribute to Belle, Michael Laing and all the Housing staff and workforce who worked hard to achieve our two stars. It was so sad when Belle died in September 2004. I miss her very much.

There were lots and lots of meetings, it was a very strenuous time and very stressful. I noticed that my close friend Cllr Belle Bousefield was getting a little bit short and a bit down. I asked her if she was all right and she said she was going to the doctors. But when she did, they said she should take a rest. That was like a red rag to a bull, but – very much under protest - Belle did rest and she appeared to be alright. We had decided to try something different to the Civic Ball, which was always in February when the weather was poor, so in July 2004 we had our first "Proms in the Park" – music in the Bishop's Park. It was a beautiful setting. I went with Belle and we had a really good evening. There was a meal and then an orchestral concert in the Park. But at the end of the meal Belle came to me and said she was going home because she felt a bit tired. Since the death of Belle's husband, I would ring her every night just to see if she was alright. But on this one occasion I didn't ring her. The reason was I thought she was tired and that I would let her sleep. When Belle left that evening, the last thing she said was: 'see you tomorrow at the meeting'. However, Belle didn't turn up for the meeting, which I thought was odd. I rang her and got no reply, so I thought 'oh, she must be on her way over'. However, there was still no sign of Belle and I was getting worried. I rang her again and again, and still there was no reply. Chief Housing Officer Michael Lang also rang Belle, also to no avail, so he and his secretary Glynis Lyons decided they would go down to Belle's house to see if she was all right. When Glynis and Michael got to the house they found that Belle had died in her sleep.

Belle's sudden death shook me absolutely rigid. She was my best friend, and she and I got on like a house on fire. We argued in the Council Chamber quite a lot, but that's what friendships are about - being able to agree to disagree. I was absolutely gutted by Belle's death and it really knocked me sideways. In the midst of life, there is death. That was one thing that I felt really upset about. It took me quite a while to get over Belle's death, in fact I still think about her every day. Belle was a tremendous personality, extremely hard-working. The best thing that I could think of to commemorate her was that we should go on to get the two stars for our Housing Service, and this we did.

Coup d'Etat

I continued with my work in Europe on the Committee of the Regions. I thoroughly enjoyed the time that I had in Europe, but it was perhaps at a cost to myself and to my Leadership of the Council because unfortunately, in 2005, I

"Is this a dagger I see before me?" "No, it's behind you!"

was the victim of a "Coup d'Etat". Some of the Labour Councillors clearly thought I wasn't capable of doing the job as Council Leader – although I had done it successfully for ten years – perhaps others thought I was spending too much time in Europe. Other Council Leaders were managing to do both jobs – why not me? If only the people who wanted me out had come to me and asked me, I could well have agreed to step down. I had been thinking of giving up the Leadership while keeping up my European work. But no, they decided to remove me from the Leadership behind my back. I thought to myself: 'if that's the way they want it that's it, let them have it'. I decided not to stand for the Council again in the 2007 elections - I had had enough. Ironically, I had already made my mind up long before what happened to me in 2005 that I would just take a seat on the back-benches for my last year as a Councillor. So in fact I did enjoy my last 18 months on the Council because I could look around and watch what was going on without the pressures of leadership. People wondered why I was removed as Leader, but I never commented. I thought: 'no, you wanted it, get on with the job and that's it'. It is sad and indeed a fault with people who refused to negotiate, and why they take this attitude I don't know. *[Chris: for the record, Cllr Neil Stonehouse, Olive's deputy, took over as Labour Group and Council Leader, with Cllr Charlie Kay as his deputy].*

Unfortunately, at the 2007 elections the Labour Party lost its majority and was reduced to 18 seats (later down to 17 when one Labour Councillor became an Independent). The Liberal Democrats got 16 and the Independents six, so it was a very tight election. It wasn't going to be an easy couple of last years for the Labour Party on the Council, but that was their look-out. After the election the Labour Party did again take control of the Council, although it had to rely on support from the Independents. I don't know what happened, and I don't want to know, but perhaps the Independents got tired of the Labour Group's attitude because they are not used to being told what to do. I think the Labour Group got a little bit too dictatorial and therefore the Independents said: 'that's it, we are having no more of you'. So in the final year of Wear Valley Council, 2008/2009, the Labour Party found itself out of power and the Liberal Democrats are now running the council. *[Chris: again for the record, the minority LibDem administration at first had Cllr Tommy Taylor as Leader. He was later replaced as Leader by Cllr Neil Harrison, with Cllr Sam Zair continuing as Deputy Leader].*

Chapter Nineteen

Chris: I will never quit

Honorary Alderman; Politics is in my blood

Honorary Alderman

But I want to end on a happy and optimistic note. I thoroughly enjoyed my 40 years as a local councillor and I don't regret a moment of it. So it was extremely pleasing when the Council voted unanimously (Labour, LibDem and Independents) to make me an Honorary Alderman of Wear Valley, along with Olive Brown, for whom I have the greatest respect despite our political differences. It was an equal pleasure later to be made an Honorary Alderman of Durham County as well. A double Alderman – that's great.

What might have been – CFW as "JR"

Politics is in my blood

But I remain active in politics and always will, as long as I draw breath. Politics is in my blood and has been a well-spring for me throughout my life. To me, there is no finer calling than public service. After being prevented from standing for the new County Council in Bishop Auckland in 2008 by members of my own Party, I helped the Party by standing (although without success) in Newton Aycliffe. In June 2009 I am again contesting the European elections as No.2 on the LibDem list for the North East. I remain on the "active" list of approved parliamentary candidates, and I still represent the North East on national and European Party bodies (which I attend largely at my own expense). As to my professional work, I now earn my living as a full-time author, editor and publisher of non-fiction books, particularly biographies. I travel widely, researching my books and giving "Author Talks". There are also several non-profit making books I intend to write about politics and political figures in the North East, to add to my 2002 book "Land of 100 Quangos", my expose of the 100+ unelected, government-appointed bodies who run this region.

I will always be grateful to the people of Bishop Auckland and the Dene Valley who put their trust in me by voting for me over the past forty years. I always did my best for the people I represented, for the District as a whole, and for the North East, and I know I never betrayed their trust.

Chapter Twenty

Olive: Ending on a High Note

Honorary Alderman; Queen's Birthday Honours; Political correctness;
Proud of my Record; "Je ne regrette rien"

Honorary Alderman

Since I was removed as Leader of the Council, two wonderful things have happened to me. First, I was made an Honorary Alderman of Wear Valley by the District Council on the 25th June 2007, along with Cllr Foote Wood, both for our long service to the Council, in my case 37 years and in his case 40 years. That made me feel very happy indeed. At least the Council had appreciated both of us for our long service. With John Richardson, we are the only three Honorary Aldermen appointed by Wear Valley to date.

Queen's Birthday Honours

The thing that made it an extra-special year for me was that in the Queen's Birthday Honours list 2007 I was awarded the MBE. I was absolutely thrilled and indeed flabbergasted. The great many letters and kind comments I have had from people from all walks of life, many of whom I've known for years, made me feel very happy that people had appreciated my work as a Councillor. In particular, the people of Crook in large numbers have stopped me in the street and congratulated me. I got comments like: 'Olive, there's one thing about you, you told it as it was, you never embroidered anything and that's why we are over the moon for you. I thought that was a wonderful commendation from the people I had represented all of those years. I was very touched by it and even now they stop me in the street and say 'are you alright pet, are you ok, all right, enjoying your retirement?' and so on.

And so we went to Buckingham Palace again on October 10th 2007, this time for me to receive my MBE from the Queen. It was a wonderful experience, but it was also sad for me because I knew my parents would have been so proud of me. Ken came with me and also my friend Diane from Belgium who had set me off in politics all those years ago. I took Diane as well because I thought she deserved to come and see me get my MBE because it was with her help that I went into politics. She has helped me ever since. We've always talked about things, and for me, looking at something from another point of view sometimes makes it easier to understand. But I must say that I do thank the people of Crook who I've represented for 37 years. I really appreciate their thoughts. I think that living in Crook all my life and being well-known has certainly helped me in my political career.

Political correctness

I want to talk a little light heartedly now about political correctness. I joined the Labour Party many years ago because I felt it was a reforming Party and had a lot to offer. Also, when Tony Blair came into power I was also very interested in reforming the Labour Party. So I was very pleased when we did start to reform, however, this political correctness is something else. Somebody once asked me if I was politically correct. I said I've never been politically correct in my life but I've never broken the law, I've always used common-sense. I think instead of creating political correctness, common-sense should have been the guide as to what is best. We should not be guided by strict rules and regulations. I don't believe in political correctness, I believe in people because people are what matter in my life and always have been and always will be. It's time that politicians realised that they are there to represent the views of the people, for the people, of the people and by the people and not go off into silly little avenues like political correctness. That's my view and it will not change.

I was Leader of Wear Valley Council for ten years, I made lots of friends and met many interesting people. I enjoyed every minute of my life as a Councillor for 37 years. When I was Leader, I got on well with all the staff and workforce. I told them my door was always open to see them if they had any problems. I could see things from both sides, as I had been a union rep for Nalgo (now part of Unison) during my working days with the Library Service [Chris: I was Branch Secretary of Nalgo when I worked for Bishop Auckland UDC]. At the moment I am busy being involved in the setting-up of a Town Council for Crook.

Proud of my Record

I am very proud of my record as Leader of WVDC. I led the Labour Party to three election victories in Wear Valley in 1995, 1999 and 2003. I had already decided to retire before the 2007 elections, and I was going to inform the Labour Group of my decision not to contest the next election. However, they removed me as Leader. It is most ironic in the 2007 elections that Labour lost its majority on the Council, and it was very sad to see this happen, especially in the last years of Wear Valley Council's existence. There is one thing I can say: I tried my best as Leader of Wear Valley District Council, and I was happy and proud to serve the people of Wear Valley both as Leader and as a Councillor.

"Je ne regrette rien"

I'm still very interested in Europe and always will be. I think our country should have played a much bigger role in Europe from the start. I know a lot of people will disagree with me, but I think we should try and look at other people and not be so inward-looking. With all these crises that are happening now, I'm still interested in politics and always will be. The way the world is going at the moment, we just don't know what's going to happen. People are worrying about rising prices, rising fuel prices, rising energy costs and also food prices, not to mention bank failures, the collapse of the housing market, the "credit crunch" and rising unemployment , but as a country we have come through difficult times before and succeeded and will do so again. I have met a lot of very interesting people and made many friends from all over the world, and for that I am really grateful. I will finish in the words of one of my favourite singers, Edith Piaf. For me it's still and will always be "JE NE REGRETTE RIEN".